MEETING
OF MINDS

MEETING OF MINDS

The complete scripts, with illustrations, of the
amazingly successful PBS-TV series.

FIRST SERIES

STEVE ALLEN

PROMETHEUS BOOKS • BUFFALO, NEW YORK

Library of Congress Card Catalogue Number: 89-62786

*To my wife, Jayne, without whose
invaluable assistance as researcher,
editor, and actress I could not have
brought "Meeting of Minds" to fruition.*

CONTENTS

An insert of photographs follows page 86

MEETING
OF
MINDS

INTRODUCTION

The Story of "Meeting of Minds"

I LOVE TO READ. BUT THIS LOVE, LIKE OTHERS MEN MAY know, is in part a compulsion. I am powerless to resist the temptation to read. I perceive the magic, wondrous power of reading, and it disturbs me that many others do not share this insight. The great majority on our planet, which not very long ago we imagined was generally civilized, is still illiterate. These damnable polysyllabic words, such as *illiterate*, serve as mental filing devices but obscure the reality they were intended to convey. Think for a moment, really think, what it means to be unable to read. Of course we are all relatively illiterate in the sense that though there are hundreds of languages in the world, even many educated people can read only one and perhaps an additional one or two stumblingly. But hundreds of millions, even in the twentieth century, can read nothing at all. This means that much of the best of human achievement, from all cultures, down through the long march of history, is largely closed to them. If they happen to live within walking distance of an ancient temple, a great cathedral, a sculpture by Michelange-lo, a painting by da Vinci, if they are able to hear a performance of a symphony by Brahms or Beethoven, they are fortunate indeed, but few illiterates are so situated. And the degrading, dehumanizing social circumstances which may have contrib-uted to their illiteracy make it extremely unlikely that they will avail themselves of even such opportunities as might present themselves. For the man who cannot read, Dostoevski and

1

Bacon might as well have lived on another planet, Aristotle and
Aquinas might as well have never been born.

So far as can be scientifically determined the important
difference between man and the other thousands of animal
species is that man thinks analytically and remembers. Reading, writing, printing, and publishing are extensions of this one
fundamental difference. But if the ignorance that illiteracy
invariably leads to is pathetic, tragic, what can one say of those
who possess the gift of literacy but essentially waste it solely for
purposes of diversion, practically never use it with an eye to
enlightenment, moral betterment, or social responsibility? The
child has at least an excuse for reading little more than comic
strips, advertisements, or simple stories. But what of a college
graduate who reads chiefly sensational tabloids, sports news,
pornography, commercial advertisements, and the other forms
of mindless fare produced in such enormous quantities by our
culture because someone can turn a profit from it?

Well, all of this seems monumentally tragic to me; I therefore
consider myself fortunate that I am seized by reading, as a
result of which I am in a constant lifelong state of intellectual
and/or creative excitement. I find no subject matter more
stimulating than philosophy and history although I am willing,
at rare intervals, to read a spy thriller or watch the visual
equivalent on television.

To say that this endless reading is the *source* of many of my
ideas would suggest that I simply find in books and articles
ideas of others and take them as my own. No, my mind does
not simply receive impressions. It talks back to the authors,
even the wisest of them, a response I'm sure they would warmly
welcome. It is not possible, after all, to accept passively everything even the greatest minds have proposed. One naturally has
profound respect for Socrates, Plato, Pascal, Augustine, Des-
cartes, Newton, Locke, Voltaire, Paine, and other heroes of
the pantheon of Western culture; but each made statements
flatly contradicted by views of the others. So I see the literary
and philosophical tradition of our culture not so much as a
storehouse of facts and ideas but rather as a hopefully endless
Great Debate at which one may be not only a privileged listener
but even a modest participant. It was this last perception that
led to the creation of "Meeting of Minds."

*

After three years as host of NBC's original "Tonight Show," in 1954, 1955, and 1956, I had been assigned to produce a second program, a weekly prime-time comedy series, which the network carried for four years. On this program I from time to time referred briefly to books I thought deserved a wider audience.

By 1959 it had become clear that certain network and advertising people were made politically uneasy by the weekly recommendations of books, even though one Sunday I publicized one written by J. Edgar Hoover, simply because my publisher had asked me to. But NBC would have preferred that I function in an intellectual vacuum, restricting myself to making audiences laugh rather than think. When I responded that it was precisely because I was able to do the former that I was in an advantageous position to accomplish the latter, the point seemed to carry little weight. The recommendation of books continued to be tolerated rather than approved. Then, in January of 1960, matters came to a head.

For some time an idea had been vaguely forming in the back of my mind of a method of imparting education without inducing boredom. In early 1959 I had made the following entry in a notebook:

> What I have in mind, however hazily, is probably a drama that would present characters embodying philosophical attitudes. Shaw and other dramatists have done something of this sort. There must be minds at hand capable of at least making this experiment.

About six months later I entered the following notation:

> If I had the time I would like to develop the vague idea that it might be worthwhile to create a television program of powerful intellectual content made attractive to the masses by virtue of being clothed in the garments of emotional conflict. Shakespeare, for example, makes us think at the same time he makes us feel. Perhaps present-day intellectuals should take a leaf from his book and try to develop a program that offers ideas in dramatic conflict. The business of debate is almost always exciting. Unfortunately our national conformist pressures

probably make it impossible to broadcast any unpopular ideas, especially since sponsors frighten easily, understandably enough. But there must be some way to take constructive advantage, intellectually, of the emotional interests of the people.

There was some prophecy as well as inspiration in these lines. By December the idea at last crystallized into "Meeting of Minds," a round-table discussion of weighty issues conducted like any other panel debate except that the participants would be actors portraying Thomas Aquinas, Abraham Lincoln, Socrates, Meister Eckhart, Emerson, and others.

One night, while leafing through the Syntopicon of the Great Books of the Western World Library, I found myself examining the chapter on crime and punishment. I was fascinated by the comparison among the ideas on this subject of Freud, Aristotle, Montaigne, Dostoevski, Hegel. I asked my friend journalist-critic Nat Hentoff to research this chapter and assemble the various viewpoints into the form of a dialogue. Within a couple of weeks we had cast such distinguished actors as Everett Sloane, J. Carrol Naish, Ian Wolfe, Lawrence Dobkin, and Phillip Coolidge in the above roles, with Henry Hull playing Clarence Darrow. Our first rehearsal was thrilling, although it revealed that the script was overly long and needed additional dramatic values. I ran it through my typewriter, brought the time down to about nineteen minutes, and shortened a few of the longer speeches by breaking them up with interruptions and angry interpolations.

Copies were sent to a number of friends. One, Norman Cousins of *Saturday Review*, reacted so favorably that he immediately planned a cover story on the subject and assigned Robert Lewis Shayon to write it.

Since by this time we had once again become aware of the familiar lack of enthusiasm on the part of some of those connected with our program, I had Norman's warm letter of response reproduced and sent to all interested parties.

At first reaction was improved, but in a few days requests began to come through that we cancel plans to broadcast the discussion. We were dumbfounded. If ever an idea had found its proper time, this was it. Television was being daily attacked by the nation's intellectuals, critics, and the public. There were good programs, a few with intellectual content, but for the most part they were relegated to the Sunday afternoon low-rated period. Here was a chance to bring something of rare value to an already guaranteed mass audience. When we heard that NBC wanted us to cut the spot, I felt as Edison might have if they had rejected the electric light while sitting in the darkness.

At first I could not take the network's objections seriously. None of the points its spokesmen made seemed valid. NBC's basic argument, that "Meeting of Minds" was not the kind of fare to present on a comedy-variety program, was easily parried. While it was true that something of this sort would seem peculiar if hosted by, say, Jerry Lewis or Red Skelton, it was not at all unusual in my own case. From my first days in television I had occasionally presented material of a serious nature. "Meeting of Minds" was not comedy, but variety is a more elastic word. A couple of years earlier, for example, Ed Sullivan had presented a pacifist film that dramatically delineated the horrors of atomic warfare. Public reaction was so favorable that a few weeks later he rebroadcast the feature. I do not recall anyone saying, "I was fascinated by the antiwar film Sullivan showed, but wasn't it a pity it was broadcast on a variety show?"

We soon became aware, by a shift in the network's arguments, that this suggested reason actually had nothing to do with the matter. It was simply what had been put to us at first in the hope that we would give in and that it would not be necessary for the network to reveal its true motivations. But within a few days we became aware that disapproval was tied to my connection with the National Committee for a Sane Nuclear Policy, as well as to having permitted the use of my name in an anti-death penalty campaign centered on the Caryl Chessman case. Although the debate was handled gingerly on the part of the network's representatives, it became clear at last that the old fear that the broadcast might antagonize potential customers was at the heart of the censorship. Our sponsor was an automobile company.

"I fail to see what is controversial about this script," I said. "Clarence Darrow does declare himself opposed to capital punishment but Hegel defends—"

"That's just it," a network man said. "Some people are going to think you prepared this script because of your feelings about Chessman."

"But that's preposterous. Until this minute it had never occurred to me that there could be any connection. Nat Hentoff put the original draft together quoting from material he found in the writings of the thinkers involved. Anybody who sees this as a pro-Chessman plot is paranoid."

"Perhaps," the executive said, "but don't you see that you can't control other people's reactions? No matter how right you are, some people are going to misunderstand."

"I see no reason to deprive twenty million viewers of something wonderfully exciting and informative," I said, "just because of what a handful of crackpots might say."

At last, having reached an impasse, I pointed out that *Saturday Review* was coming out with a cover story on "Meeting of Minds" and that if we were to cancel the segment there would be a great hue and/or cry. I felt sure the cancellation would embarrass the network, the advertising agency, and the sponsor far more than they would be discomfited by the broadcast of the dialogue. In my opinion they would not be embarrassed by the broadcast at all, but would be proud to have had a part in it.

This argument had a telling effect and put an end to the discussion, for the time being. We went ahead with our plans. The men who had been sent out from New York to induce me to alter my position said a cordial good-bye and returned home. We assumed that nothing more would be said or done about the matter, but two days later we received word from the network's legal department that according to the terms of our contract we did not have the legal right to broadcast "Meeting of Minds." There was nothing more we could do; I did not own the network. I sent Norman Cousins a letter of apology, substituted a comedy sketch, and advised the network that it could consider itself responsible for the salaries of the dismissed actors, which as I recall came to about $15,000.

As predicted, the cancellation received a great deal of attention, much more than the broadcast would have. The network, the agency, and the sponsor were subjected to bitter criticism.

Perhaps this kind of censorship will inevitably occur in television in the future because of the structure of the system, which makes all parties vulnerable in their bank accounts. The movie, radio, and TV blacklist came about, I suspect, not so much from any basic, informed revulsion for communism on the part of the television, radio, and advertising executives responsible but more from fear of a commercial boycott on the part of vigorously anti-Communist consumers.

The cancellation of "Meeting of Minds" brought in a flood of mail, including requests from individuals, schools, churches, and social groups for copies of the script. We sent them out and granted permission for various local productions around the country. I participated in one of these at a school auditorium in Los Angeles. It was tape-recorded and subsequently broadcast on the Pacifica radio stations in San Francisco, Los Angeles, and New York.

There the matter rested until 1964 at which time I was doing a nightly syndicated comedy-and-talk show for the Westinghouse Broadcasting people. They were pleased to learn of our plan to present "Meeting of Minds" in its original form. The telecast passed with nothing more earthshaking than a number of complimentary letters and reviews.

By 1971 I was doing another syndicated talk series, and this time decided to present "Meeting of Minds" in a more appropriate form, having realized that it was a mistake to limit the discussions to one subject. Even the greatest minds will tend to ramble and digress, though less so than the rest of us; this factor, I thought, would lend a more natural quality to the conversations. I wrote a totally new script bringing together President Theodore Roosevelt, St. Thomas Aquinas, Queen Cleopatra of ancient Egypt, and Thomas Paine of the American and French revolutions.

In rehearsals it developed that we had made an error in casting a certain actor to portray Paine. Under my direction his performance worsened, so he had to be dismissed. Unfortunately this left us without enough time to get another actor for the role. I therefore took it over myself and asked Peter Lawford if he would be kind enough to serve as host, a request to which he graciously consented.

The telecast was aired on a Friday. By Monday morning our office was flooded with about fifteen hundred letters from viewers who had seen the show on the Los Angeles station. I instructed our office staff to be prepared to hire additional personnel to take care of the avalanche of mail that would come in from the other cities around the country where the program was seen.

About two weeks later it occurred to us that we had seen no

additional mail, which was certainly strange. When I attempted to discover the reasons my efforts at first were met with evasions and pretended ignorance. Eventually it emerged that the gentleman serving as distributor for the show had taken it upon himself to censor it from our entire network of syndicated stations, with the exception of our Los Angeles outlet. He reasoned, cleverly enough, that if we saw the show in Los Angeles we would have no way of knowing that it was not simultaneously being carried throughout the rest of the country. He would have gotten away with this, too, had it not been for the factor of the congratulatory mail.

The disaster, however, turned out to have fortunate consequences. Since the program had been only a local show it was entered, by our executive producer Loring d'Usseau, in the local competition sponsored by the National Academy of TV Arts and Sciences. In due course it won three Emmy awards.

On the strength of this reassurance I financed the production of six additional one-hour programs and attempted to sell them to syndicators or networks. One by one various doors were opened and then unaccountably closed. Compliments were lavish but . . . no sale.

The only remaining hope seemed to be PBS, the "educational" network. Perhaps the most surprising turn of events of the whole long history of the "Meeting of Minds" project is that . . . well, it's not totally correct to say that the network turned the series down. Statistically very few people there ever became aware it had been submitted. But a couple of gentlemen in one of the eastern PBS cities decided, for reasons never made clear, that they weren't interested.

Having exhausted all evident possibilities I simply concentrated on other creative projects. "Meeting of Minds" would have been added to the list of thousands of other unsold TV "pilots" had it not been for an accident of fate. Shortly thereafter Loring d'Usseau, who had been executive producer when we did the 1971 telecast, happened to leave the Los Angeles NBC station and move to KCET, the local outlet for PBS, as program manager. Since Loring had received one of the three Los Angeles Emmys the program had won, it was obvious that he would not have to be sold on the project. I wrote him and he responded with immediate enthusiasm. Because the six scripts were already written we were, in a word, ready to go.

There was just one remaining problem: PBS has no money of its own but must seek funding for its programs. Fortunately a gentleman named William Clayton, an executive of E. F. Hutton and Co., saw one of our pilot tapes and became instantly enamored of the whole idea. Between Messrs. d'Usseau and Clayton they made it possible to proceed with the production of our first group of shows, six one-hour specials, the first of which was telecast nationally on January 10, 1977.

*

The program was, after a delay of some eighteen years, not only enormously successful but elicited a kind of mail none of us connected with its production had ever seen. What appealed to the thousands who wrote, I believe, was that they were actually given the opportunity to hear *ideas* on television, a medium which otherwise presents only people, things, and actions.

We certainly desperately need to become more familiar with such ideas. Modern man is going to have to examine the historical roots of modern practices if he is to even approach understanding them. "Meeting of Minds" encourages him to do so.

The distinctive feature of "Meeting of Minds" is that it does not consist of one-on-one interviews but rather of group discussions, stimulating conversations by important thinkers and/or doers of history. There have been other shows where Abraham Lincoln, say, was interviewed, as there have been programs in which Lincoln appeared in a dramatic context. But, except in the realm of literature, which provides much precedent, there has been nothing remotely resembling "Meeting of Minds," in which Lincoln might be joined at the table by Julius Caesar, Henry VIII, and Aristotle. As host I spend the least possible amount of time interviewing our guests because the real excitement comes from their heated disagreements with each other.

It's important to note that the guests could never have met in reality, perhaps because they lived a thousand years or a thousand miles apart. Having George Washington speaking to Thomas Jefferson and James Madison wouldn't be all that surprising, but hearing him debate important questions with

Augustine, Freud, and Lenin would be, at the very least, instructive.

I should not want the casual reader to assume—or the scholar to imagine I intended—that the scant bits and pieces of information about the personages from history here introduced represent even an adeqate scratching of their mountainous surfaces. Historians have nothing whatever to learn from the present work, although they might be amused at seeing separate ideas with which they are already familiar brought into abrasive contact. But the book, like the television program, is intended for the layman who, sad to say, is historically illiterate. I do not refer here to the average man's ignorance of the proper names of ancient battles, the birth dates and death dates of important players in the drama of history, the details of obscure and no-longer-significant controversies. That most of us have little knowledge of such things is perhaps of no great moment, but it is disturbing that we know so little of those important philosophical elements of our history that have created the fabric of our present. I go so far as to say that the brief and still somewhat shaky experiment with freedom is unresolved partly because of the ignorance of its presumed defenders in the West.

The following six scripts represent only a modest effort to convince American viewers, and readers, that they must personally become participants in the Great Debate.

(As rendered here, by the way, the scripts are slightly longer than the broadcast versions. Since the programs naturally had to conform to the sixty-minute limit, certain passages had to be deleted during rehearsals. Additional lines and paragraphs were eliminated while the video tapes were being edited. Some other minor additions and corrections also had to be made. The original telecasts, for example, carried an error about "the burning of witches" in New England. Women believed to be witches were indeed killed in New England but the method of execution was not burning.)

SHOW #1

President Theodore Roosevelt

(JOSEPH EARLEY)

Queen Cleopatra

(JAYNE MEADOWS)

Father Thomas Aquinas

(PETER BROMILOW)

Thomas Paine

(JOE SIROLA)

&

Steve Allen

STEVE: In the thirteenth century the great poet of Florence Dante Alighieri created one of history's literary masterpieces, *The Divine Comedy*. At the beginning of the poem Dante is welcomed at the gates of Hell by Virgil, the Latin poet. Subsequently he meets Cicero, Plato, Aristotle, and others who played important roles in history. The idea of bringing together great thinkers and important personages of the past, then, is very ancient. And it is an appealing vision. Wouldn't it be exciting if we could meet the actual flesh and blood Cleopatra, ask her questions about Julius Caesar? Wouldn't it be fascinating to discuss theology with Thomas Aquinas, revolution with Thomas Paine, or the problems of twentieth-century America with Theodore Roosevelt?

Well, by what magic I have no intention of revealing, we can.

Ladies and gentlemen, one of the most fascinating guests it's ever been my privilege to present—you know him not only from your history books, but also from Mt. Rushmore—former president, Theodore Roosevelt. *(He enters and seats himself.)* *(Superimpose: Theodore Roosevelt, 1858–1919.)*

STEVE: Mr. President, we're honored to welcome you.

ROOSEVELT: It is my pleasure, sir.

STEVE: Sir, I mentioned Mt. Rushmore. Do you like the bust of you on the side of the famous mountain?

ROOSEVELT: *(He chuckles.)* Well, I'm naturally honored to be included in such distinguished company, but I've always felt the likeness makes me look a little heavier than I thought I was. I always kept myself in very good trim, you know.

STEVE: Yes, so we've heard. In brief sir, what was your political background before you became president?

ROOSEVELT: Well, Mr. Allen, I was assemblyman of the state of New York; Civil Service commissioner in Washington, D.C.; police commissioner of New York City; and assistant secretary of the Navy.

STEVE: After that came your adventures with the "Rough Riders" in the Spanish-American War?

ROOSEVELT: Yes, that's right. I then became governor of New York State. While governor of New York, I was elected vice president under McKinley. Then, when McKinley was assassinated I became the youngest president to hold office.

STEVE: I hadn't realized that.

ROOSEVELT: Yes, I was forty-three at the time. I was then elected president in my own right, in 1904.

STEVE: To go back a bit earlier in your career, Mr. President, what were some of the problems you faced when you were head of the Police Board in New York? Were they at all the same as now?

ROOSEVELT: Yes, to some extent. In my day, too, there was crime in the streets, violence, fraud, and even police corruption.

STEVE: Oh, really?

ROOSEVELT: Yes, I had to replace Chief of Police Byrne. He owned a $150,000 home on Long Island which, I'm sure, he did not buy on his police pay.

We even had a great many racial problems, including anti-Semitism.

STEVE: Is that right?

ROOSEVELT: I recall one story you might enjoy.

STEVE: Try me and see.

ROOSEVELT: There was a German preacher, a Rector Ahlwardt, who had come over to this country and was preaching anti-Semitism. Of course wherever he appeared he was picketed loudly by our American Jews. So he came to me and demanded police protection. Well, I had to give him protection, under the law, but I thought I solved the problem quite well.

STEVE: How was that?

ROOSEVELT: I assigned him forty Jewish policemen and a Jewish sergeant!

STEVE: You were born just prior to the Civil War, Mr. President. Do you have any particular memories of that period?

ROOSEVELT: Well, Mr. Allen, during the Civil War of course I was just a young boy of six or seven years old, but I was aware of what was going on. My father was a merchant and also a collector at the Port of New York City. He was quite involved with the Union Cause.

Well, what is interesting is that my mother, a lovely and gracious woman, was Martha Bullock. She had been born in Roswell, Georgia, and, of course, was an avid sympathizer of the Confederate cause. One of her brothers, in fact, was an admiral in the Confederate Navy.

STEVE: So you experienced the disagreements of the Civil War right in your own home.

ROOSEVELT: Quite so. Now during the Civil War we lived on Twentieth Street in lower Manhattan, and we had a balcony outside the second floor window. I remember one afternoon my mother hung the Confederate flag over the balcony railing . . . much to my father's chagrin and that of the shouting, fist-waving crowd below! She caused a near riot, but one must admit she did have spirit.

STEVE: In just a moment, Mr. President, we're going to bring out that very spirited lady Queen Cleopatra of Egypt. I don't suppose she'll intimidate you?

ROOSEVELT: *(He laughs good-naturedly.)* Goodness, no. Fascinating woman! I must ask her how she feels about the subject that all of you seem to be talking about these days, women's liberation.

STEVE: Ah. How do you feel about it?

ROOSEVELT: Well, I've always thought that a woman should have the same rights as a man, and in this country she must. Women in my day, you know, responded wonderfully to my progressive campaigns. Perhaps they have a more sensitive awareness of social injustice than men.

I am reminded, in this connection, that one of the noblest chapters in the history of our country was written by that wonderful woman who conducted the affairs of Hull House in Chicago. I refer, of course, to Jane Addams.

You know, it has always seemed to me disgraceful that those who are motivated by charitable concern for the well-being of their fellow citizens are often described by heartless people as "do-gooders" or "bleeding hearts." I was so described myself. But what we must realize is that our society needs *more* do-gooders.

STEVE: Well now, Mr. President, that's a very pretty sentiment, but I wonder if perhaps you're not guilty of inconsistency here.

In 1906 I understand that you criticized the writers and journalists who were then exposing corruption in business and politics. You compared them to the muckraker in John Bunyan's *Pilgrim's Progress*.

Wouldn't it be true, sir, that those muckrakers—or crusading journalists, as they considered themselves—saw themselves as "do-gooders" and "bleeding hearts"?

ROOSEVELT: Well, yes, I suppose so. This may be one of those questions of whose ox is being gored. I naturally wasn't in favor of corruption, in either business or politics, but I did think that some of the writers you refer to went too far! They seemed

to delight in offering sensational and gossipy details, although
I concede that such judgments are a matter of opinion.

STEVE: Well, forgive the interruption. You had started to mention
Jane Addams.

ROOSEVELT: Yes, she was one of the greatest do-gooders of all
time. She established Chicago's famous Hull House in 1889,
for the sole purpose of helping women, children, and
immigrants find their useful place in society.

She and her friends campaigned tirelessly against sweat-
shop conditions and child labor, and it was very largely
through Jane Addams's efforts that the Illinois State Legislature passed the first Factory Law prohibiting the employ-
ment of children below the age of fourteen.

That law fixed an eight-hour day for women, and also
provided for factory inspections of labor conditions by the
state.

STEVE: Well, Mr. President, you make that sound like some sort
of incredible achievement. Who on earth could possibly have
opposed such a law?

ROOSEVELT: The answer, Mr. Allen, is that practically *everybody*
in power at that time opposed such civilized and humane laws.

STEVE: Really?

ROOSEVELT: Yes! The masses of people naturally wanted better
conditions, but the ruling powers resisted such progressive
legislation for as long as they could get away with it. And I am
astounded to observe that today, half a century later, they still
seem to be getting away with it here and there!

You know, it was no easy matter in those days to force big
business to maintain clean factories and packing plants and give
the most careful consideration to the question of public health.

Sad to say, exactly the *opposite* was the case. The manufacturers of many of our products were interested in nothing whatever but making money. We really had to fight hard to pass the
Pure Food and Drug Act and the Meat Inspection Amendment
to the Agricultural Appropriations Act.

STEVE: Good for you, sir.

ROOSEVELT: Well, much of the work was done by a courageous man
named Dr. Harvey Wiley. He was the chief chemist in the
Department of Agriculture, a mountain among men. He
worked long and hard for a law to prevent the manufacture and
sale of adulterated or poisonous food and drugs.

I gave him a great deal of help, if I do say so myself, and his bill finally came to the floor of the Senate in the spring of 1906.

STEVE: You mean to say, Mr. President, that there were actually forces in the nation at that time that *opposed* such laws?

ROOSEVELT: Well, yes, of course. The manufacturers of the food and drug products didn't want such laws; and they had their paid allies in the Congress: Senator Nelson Aldrich of Rhode Island sneered at the arguments of Dr. Wiley and said that the liberty of all people was at stake.

But wiser heads prevailed. Senator Porter McCumber of North Dakota pointed out that the public had a right to receive what it asked for, and paid for, instead of some poisonous substitute.

But perhaps the most exciting fight of all was for the Meat Inspection Amendment. I confess that I didn't know much about the problem until I read Upton Sinclair's great novel, *The Jungle*. You young people ought to read that book today because a lot of what it said applies to some problems you face now.

Because I have always admired the book, I brought a copy of it along with me; and I'd like to quote a relevant portion of it to you now:

> There was never the least attention paid to what was cut up for sausage; there would come all the way back from Europe old sausage that had been rejected, and that was moldy and white, it would be doused with borax and glycerine and dumped into the hoppers, and made over for home consumption.
>
> There would be meat that had tumbled out on the floor, in the dirt and sawdust, where the workers had tramped and spit uncounted millions of germs . . . a man could run his hand over these piles of meat and sweep off handfuls of the dried dung of rats.

So much for the conscience of those who were selling this poisonous swill to the unsuspecting people of America.

STEVE: What accusations were made against you, Mr. President, when you tried to protect the public in this controversy?

ROOSEVELT: Oh, we were all called Socialists, among other things.

STEVE: Of what other campaigns are you now particularly proud, Mr. President?

ROOSEVELT: Well, you people today are very rightly concerned about preserving your natural resources and preserving the wilderness areas. That was a very important battle in my day, too.

In 1905 I rehabilitated the Bureau of Forestry, renaming it the Forest Service; and, if I do say so myself, it was a great move.

The new agency, you see, was staffed with trained and dedicated *foresters*. Our people began tree-planting experiments. At that time the utilities corporations were arranging to have a great many bills passed permitting them to build dams almost anywhere they wanted. Well, I slowed down *that* process until the matter could be carefully studied.

In addition, I saw to it that *125 million acres* were added to the national forests. And I also persuaded the big lumber corporations to adopt selective cutting techniques so that future generations would have timber in this country.

STEVE: Well, I imagine all of this must have made you even more of a national hero.

ROOSEVELT: Don't you believe it. The people often didn't know what I was trying to do for them, and the big interests and their lackeys in Congress responded with hysterical charges. All I was trying to do was *preserve our country's national monuments, create new national forests*, and that sort of thing; but of course the real estate developers had their eyes on those lands, and they didn't like what I was doing.

STEVE: From the moral point of view, Mr. Roosevelt, you would seem to have helped enact some of the most noble legislation ever seen on the American continent. The working man is entitled to social justice but it often takes courageous statesmen such as you to secure it for him.

If you could come back to earth to stay, Mr. President, would you like to run for office again?

ROOSEVELT: *(He smiles.)* Bully for that idea, sir. I would like that very much. It would give me the opportunity to complete some unfinished business that I started long ago.

STEVE: Thank you, Mr. President.

Our next guest is one of the most remarkable women in all history. She became queen of Egypt fifty-one years before the birth of Christ, when she was only eighteen. She would have been considered unusual in any age because she was strikingly intelligent, so attractive that both Julius Caesar and the other great general Marc Antony fell in love with her; and yet she also had the instincts of a master politician. Certainly she is one of the most patriotic women in history. Her entire life was dedicated to increasing the power of her country and defending it against the threat posed by Rome. It is no wonder she has fascinated Shakespeare, Shaw, and hundreds of other authors.

Ladies and gentlemen, Her Majesty, Cleopatra, Queen of Egypt. *(Cleopatra enters. Roosevelt and Allen remain standing briefly.) (Superimpose: Cleopatra, Queen of Egypt, 69?–30 B.C.)*

STEVE: Oh, Mr. President, Her Majesty has kindly consented to dispense with the formalities befitting her station.

CLEOPATRA: Yes, gentlemen. You may be seated.

STEVE: Thank you, Your Majesty. My goodness, your jewels are breathtaking. Were any of those perhaps presents from Julius Caesar or Marc Antony?

CLEOPATRA: Oh, no. These were in the family for centuries. You see, the royal jewels of Egypt were far more glorious than anything even the rulers of Rome could have given me.

STEVE: I notice—if you'll forgive my perhaps appearing presumptuous—I notice that you're wearing quite a heavy eye makeup.

CLEOPATRA: In your opinion. We Egyptians invented makeup. We dyed our hair, too.

STEVE: I hadn't realized that. Tell me, were many of the women of ancient Egypt as attractive as you, Your Majesty?

CLEOPATRA: Thank you, sir, but I was not of native Egyptian stock. My own ancestors were Macedonian Greeks by origin.

ROOSEVELT: I wasn't aware of that.

CLEOPATRA: I'm not surprised, Mr. President. You Americans are notorious for your lack of interest in history.

STEVE: Oh-oh. I think there may be trouble between these two.

Well, if you'll forgive our ignorance, Your Majesty, I wonder if you could tell us what other famous figures of history were contemporary with your period? Besides Caesar and Marc Antony, I mean.

CLEOPATRA: Well, there was Cicero, the great Roman orator; Virgil, the poet.

ROOSEVELT: Herod, the King of Judea, was a contemporary of yours, wasn't he, Your Majesty?

CLEOPATRA: Yes, Mr. President. Marc Antony put him into power.

STEVE: Fascinating. Which brings to mind the problem of language. Now you spoke Egyptian, of course, and yet the famous names we associate with you—most of them—were Romans. How did you communicate? How could you tell what they were thinking?

CLEOPATRA: Oh, well now I've never had any trouble telling what men were thinking.

Actually I spoke seven languages, but the international language of my time was Greek.

STEVE: I see. How many times had Caesar been married before you came into his life?

CLEOPATRA: Four times. His only child had been a daughter. In the summer of 47 B.C. I bore him a son. A beautiful child.

ROOSEVELT: I understand that you loved that boy with a passion.

CLEOPATRA: Oh, I did, Mr. President. You see, none of Caesar's other wives, though they were patricians, could have given him a son of royal blood.

STEVE: Why not?

CLEOPATRA: For the simple reason that there was no royalty in Rome. It was a Republic at the time, you'll recall.

To tell you the truth, we Egyptians always looked upon the Romans as upstarts.

STEVE: (He laughs.) The Romans were upstarts!

CLEOPATRA: Well, you see, my own people, my Greek ancestors, had ruled over the native Egyptians for more than three hundred years. I was of the line of the Ptolemies. We had ruled Egypt since the time of Alexander the Great.

ROOSEVELT: So you had planned that your son, Caesar's son, would one day rule over what exactly?

CLEOPATRA: Over the whole known world at the time, Mr. President. My son, you see, would have been a Pharaoh, and as such his royal roots would have gone back even beyond the time of the Ptolemies.

The Pharaoh's tombs—you know some of them as the Pyramids—were ancient even in my day.

ROOSEVELT: The attitude toward royalty in our world today, Your Majesty, has sometimes very little respect to it.

CLEOPATRA: Yes, Mr. President, and more's the pity. I was treated not only as a queen but literally as a goddess. My people believed that I was the human form of the Holy Mother Isis. My son, Caesarion, little Caesar, was considered to be the son of the great God of Egypt, Amen.

STEVE: Now let me see if I have this straight, Your Majesty. You were Caesar's fifth wife, is that correct?

CLEOPATRA: Yes.

STEVE: Were you married before Caesar?

CLEOPATRA: Certainly.

STEVE: To whom?

CLEOPATRA: To my brother.

ROOSEVELT: What? You were married to your own brother?

CLEOPATRA: Of course. You see, such marriages were arranged by the Egyptian government. It was the custom. Rather than risk having us as rival claimants to the throne it was assumed that, if we married each other, we would rule together.

ROOSEVELT: Disgraceful.

STEVE: Yes, that does seem shocking to us today. Sounds rather like one of our X-rated movies.

CLEOPATRA: Really? Well, many things of your century seem shocking to me.

ROOSEVELT: Oh? Can you give us an illustration, Your Majesty?

CLEOPATRA: Yes. I think it was perfectly idiotic of you to have freed your slaves.

ROOSEVELT: What!

CLEOPATRA: There has never been a more efficient method for getting work done than slavery.

STEVE: Incredible.

CLEOPATRA: Do you think it would have been possible for my people to build the Pyramids—one of the wonders of even the modern world—if we had had to pay wages to all the hundreds of thousands of workers? Today not only do you pay your workers, but you indulge in the even more asinine practice of permitting them to organize on their own behalf, so that their wages increase almost daily.

Mark my words, gentlemen, you will eventually cause economic chaos in the Western world if you continue to permit the workers to act only out of their own self-interest!

STEVE: Perhaps I'd better change the subject. . . . Er . . . just how long did the Roman culture last?

CLEOPATRA: Only about a thousand years.

STEVE: "Only" a thousand years?

CLEOPATRA: Well, the civilization of Egypt, on the other hand, lasted as long as five thousand years.

I don't wish to downgrade the achievements of Rome. They were considerable. You might say that the Romans were the Americans of their day.

ROOSEVELT: And just what do you mean by that?

CLEOPATRA: Well, they didn't create a great deal, Mr. President. The Greeks were the true innovators—in philosophy, mathematics, sculpture, architecture. The Romans merely borrowed—from the Greeks, the Egyptians, the Etruscans, and others. Their chief contribution to the culture of your world today lay in taking what they had learned and distributing this knowledge throughout the lands that they conquered. Because the Romans were good politicians and good soldiers, and for the most part they ruled their subject peoples with considerable intelligence.

STEVE: I see. Now, just how did Julius Caesar come to rule the Roman Empire?

CLEOPATRA: Well, he had been a great general. The Roman Senate, you see, was always a somewhat shaky institution, considered as a ruling body. Caesar formed an alliance with another general, Pompey the Great, and an officer named Crassus. The three officers, you see, were displeased with the way the Senate had treated them. But after Crassus died in battle, in the year you would call 53 B.C., Pompey and Caesar became enemies.

In 49 B.C. Pompey persuaded the Senate to order Caesar to disband his army. Caesar naturally refused.

I understand you have a common expression, "crossing the Rubicon"? Well, the Rubicon River was the southern limit of Caesar's legitimate area of command. He came down out of Gaul, crossed the river—against the orders of the Senate—and marched on Rome itself. He broke through and chased the armies of Pompey all the way to Egypt.

STEVE: Did he capture him?

CLEOPATRA: No. When Pompey landed he was killed on the spot by agents of my brother Ptolemy.

ROOSEVELT: Your husband, you mean.

CLEOPATRA: Yes, husband, brother, whatever. Anyway, I met Caesar shortly thereafter.

ROOSEVELT: What kind of man was Julius Caesar?

CLEOPATRA: Caesar? Oh, there's no one like him in your time. Intellectually he was remarkable. He was a great military commander, a skillful political manipulator, and he had a good head for money. He was an able author too, as all of you know who have had to translate his *Commentaries* in school. "Omnia Gallia in tres partes divisa est."

ROOSEVELT: All Gaul is divided into three parts. (Harvard.)

STEVE: When you and Caesar met did he become . . . er . . . interested in you right from the start?

CLEOPATRA: To use your modern expression, it was love-at-first-sight.

STEVE: Was it love-at-first-sight for you, too?

CLEOPATRA: Frankly, no. Oh, I was naturally impressed by the great Caesar. As I've told you, he was a great man, and he was enormously attractive. But I confess that my interest in him initially was based on what he could do for my country.

STEVE: What were the circumstances leading to Caesar's death?

CLEOPATRA: Well, some members of the Roman Senate were jealous of Caesar, because of his power. As you know, Cassius induced Brutus to take part in a conspiracy that was forming against Caesar; and on the ides of March in 44 B.C., he was stabbed to death when he entered a meeting of the Senate.

Think of it, gentlemen. He had ruled the Roman Empire for only six months.

ROOSEVELT: Did he really say "Et tu, Brute?" You, too, Brutus?

CLEOPATRA: Indeed. He had always been very fond of Brutus, you see. It was my own belief that Brutus was in fact his illegitimate son.

STEVE: I never knew that.

CLEOPATRA: I'm not surprised.

STEVE: Well, you've told us a great deal about Caesar. If he was such a great man, it's still not clear why he was assassinated.

CLEOPATRA: Oh, Mr. Allen, that strikes me as a strange question coming from an American. Your nation, I understand, has in recent years seen three of its important men assassinated.

ROOSEVELT: Once Caesar was dead I suppose you no longer had any reason to stay in Rome.

CLEOPATRA: That's right. I took my small son and returned to Egypt. You see, when Caesar was killed a great many things died, among them the dream of a world empire that Julius and I had shared.

STEVE: Thank you, Your Majesty.

Our next guest is a truly unusual figure, even in this august company. He is regarded as one of the great philosophers of history, though he saw himself not as a philosopher but as a theologian. He lived in an age when faith was very powerful and reason was held in lower regard. Perhaps because he took faith for granted, he preached the power of reason.

Although his philosophy—six centuries later in 1879—was proclaimed the official philosophy of the Catholic Church, believe it or not, in his own day, the thirteenth century, his views were regarded by many of his fellow churchmen as a terrible collection of heresies!

Here is the dangerous radical of the thirteenth century, Father Thomas Aquinas. *(He enters and looks about, before seating himself.)* *(Superimpose: Thomas Aquinas, 1225–1274.)*

STEVE: We're honored to have you here, Father Aquinas.

AQUINAS: It is my pleasure to address your audience, Mr. Allen. Good heavens, what wonders might have been worked in my day had we been able to address millions in an instant, as you can now.

STEVE: Ah, yes. In what year were you born, Father?

AQUINAS: In 1225, in a small town near Naples.

CLEOPATRA: Ah, you were Italian. A descendant of the Romans.

AQUINAS: No, Your Majesty. Although I spent many of my years in Italy, my people were German and Norman. My father, Count Landolf of Aquina, belonged to the German nobility, and my mother was descended from the Norman princes that ruled Sicily at the time.

ROOSEVELT: Father, we've heard that as a student you were called "the dumb ox." Is that correct?

AQUINAS: *(He laughs.)* I'm afraid it is, Mr. President. Oh, I don't recall being all that dumb, but from the very first I was rather slow and, shall we say, methodical in getting a grasp of a subject. And in my early days I preferred thinking to speaking.

STEVE: I see. Where did you receive your early schooling?

AQUINAS: At the Abbey of Monte Cassino, Mr. Allen. I understand that it was destroyed in your Second World War.

ROOSEVELT: Yes, it's a pity that the Abbey was attacked.

STEVE: It has since been restored.

AQUINAS: Yes, Mr. President, but Monte Cassino was, I assure you, quite accustomed to attack. In my day, you see, it was a fortress as well as a monastery. It was taken and plundered on a number of occasions, although it was never subjected to such awesome weapons as are known in the present day.

In any event, at the age of fourteen I moved to the University of Naples.

STEVE: Was it a great university in those days?

AQUINAS: Oh, yes. The intellectual climate was most stimulating.

The philosophy of Aristotle was taught at the university. The culture of ancient Greece was very influential, you see, as were Arabic and Hebraic influences.

STEVE: I suppose your family was happy that you decided to become a priest at so early an age?

AQUINAS: *(He laughs.)* On the contrary, they were horrified.

STEVE: Really?

AQUINAS: Yes. I thought they would never stop arguing with me. The situation became so serious that when I entered the Dominican Order my mother actually sent two of my brothers to kidnap me. I was taken to our family castle at Roccasecca and kept more or less a prisoner there, for about a year.

STEVE: Incredible!

AQUINAS: But my mind was made up, and my family eventually released me. I continued my education in Paris and had the great good fortune to study under Albertus Magnus *(to Cleopatra)*, Albert the Great.

STEVE: Her Majesty speaks fluent Latin, Father.

AQUINAS: *(He smiles.)* It was at about this time that the "dumb ox" business came up, Mr. President, but Albert kindly defended me against my critics.

ROOSEVELT: Was yours an exciting age to live in, Father?

AQUINAS: Oh, tremendously so. Europe had come out of what are now called the Dark Ages. There was beginning to be some mitigation of barbarism and depravity, and conditions were im   .ng for many people. The Feudal Age was by no means w .out its faults, but it was certainly not without its merit. 'crhaps most important of all, the Christian faith began to :em less forbidding and pessimistic than it had in earlier .nturies and began to be transformed into a more reasonable and appealing doctrine. I suppose I was in a measure responsible for such evolution, although St. Francis and Pope Innocent III must also be mentioned in this connection.

ROOSEVELT: How did it come about, Father, that the combating of heresy was your particular task?

AQUINAS: Well, you see, Mr. Roosevelt, in the Church at that time, as in the present day, there were many religious orders.

STEVE: Tell us about them.

AQUINAS: Well, there were, for example, the Benedictines, named after St. Benedict, who established monasteries across the face of Europe, in which the lamp of learning was kept bright when it might otherwise have gone out. There were the Carthusians, who lived by a remarkably strict set of rules. Each Carthusian monk lived a life of poverty in a cell, fasted three days of each week on bread and water alone. They wore painful hair shirts and spent literally all their time in prayer, meditation, and manual labor.

CLEOPATRA: You mean they were slaves.

AQUINAS: Oh, no, Your Majesty.

CLEOPATRA: But they lived like slaves.

AQUINAS: With one important distinction. The Carthusians decided to live such lives. Slaves had no choice.

Then there was the Cistercian Order. By the middle of the twelfth century more than three hundred Cistercian monasteries throughout western Europe were receiving many converts to the faith.

STEVE: Three hundred monasteries?

AQUINAS: Yes. And there were the Franciscans, the followers of Francis of Assissi. The friars of St. Francis were originally not just another kind of monk but were laymen who did not shut themselves up in monasteries but spent much time preaching what today would, I suppose, be called the social gospel.

ROOSEVELT: Good for them.

AQUINAS: Yes, they did admirable social welfare work, along with their preaching and teaching of the faith. Like Francis himself, they sought to make the world a more pleasant place in which to live.

Lastly, there was my own order, the Dominicans. We were founded in the year 1215 by St. Dominic, a Castilian noble who lived at the time in southern France. The Dominicans took upon themselves the task of combating heresy. Hence it was only natural that I would specialize in that endeavor.

ROOSEVELT: I see.

(A vigorous knocking at the door is heard.)

AQUINAS: Heresy, you see, must always be—

(Again a pounding at the door.)

ROOSEVELT: What's going on?

PAINE: *(From off-stage.)* I can wait no longer, sir!

STEVE: Ah. That would be our fourth guest, Thomas Paine, I believe. Excuse me. *(He walks to the door and opens it.)* Yes. Ladies and gentlemen, Citizen Thomas Paine. *(Paine hurries in, shakes host's hand and joins others.)* *(Superimpose: Thomas Paine, 1737–1809.)*

STEVE: Mr. Paine, I wonder if—

PAINE: I beg your pardon, sir. I could overhear some of the things said by Aquinas here, and I do feel I should be present at the table so that I—

ROOSEVELT: Now, see here, Paine. You ought to wait your turn, like the rest of us!

PAINE: But Mr. President, if this man can—

STEVE: Mr. Paine, if I may, I feel I should at least formally introduce you, so that all of our viewers will be aware of your—

PAINE: Very well, sir. Say what you will. *(He acknowledges the others, who respond somewhat coldly.)* Your Majesty. Gentlemen.

STEVE: Thomas Paine was one of the truly heroic figures of the American Revolution. But because of his views on religion many have disapproved of him, among them President Theodore Roosevelt.

Mr. President, how did you describe Thomas Paine?

ROOSEVELT: I called him a dirty little atheist.

STEVE: Quite so.

PAINE: And in so doing you lied, Mr. President!

ROOSEVELT: Well, now don't you dare to—

CLEOPATRA: Gentlemen, may we *stop* this unseemly bickering and return to the subject of our conversation?

PAINE: Please do, but I shall be part of it!

CLEOPATRA: *(She turns away from Paine, who is in the chair to her right.)* Very well. Against what philosophers of your own period, Father, did you pit yourself?

AQUINAS: For a long time I was chiefly concerned in combating the views of Averroës, Your Majesty. He lived slightly before my time, but so influential was he that his opinions formed the basis for a dangerous heresy across the continent of Europe.

ROOSEVELT: Just what were the dangerous views of Averroës?

AQUINAS: He taught that the laws of nature rule the world, without any interference by God.

PAINE: Good for him!

STEVE: Which many believe today, I suppose.

AQUINAS: Alas, yes. He taught that the soul dies with the body, and he believed that heaven and hell were just fairy tales invented to encourage or terrify simple people into decency.

PAINE: I like this fellow Averroës.

ROOSEVELT: His views sound very much like those of modern man.

CLEOPATRA: Was he a Christian?

AQUINAS: Oh, no, Your Majesty. He was the most influential

philosopher of Islam, the religion of Mohammed. His home was Spain which, as you may know, was ruled by the Moors of North Africa for several centuries.

Averroës's father and grandfather had been chief justices in the city of Cordova. In 1169 Averroës himself was appointed chief justice of Seville.

CLEOPATRA: Just what kind of a man was he?

AQUINAS: As a physician he was nothing short of brilliant. For many years his encyclopaedia of medicine was widely used as a text in schools and universities simply because no Christian medical document could equal it. He contributed many important writings—not only in his commentary on Aristotle—but on logic, physics, theology, and astronomy.

PAINE: (Dryly.) And for all this you despised him?

AQUINAS: Oh, never, Mr. Paine. I opposed only his views, and not all of them.

But I should like to make a point here that modern man seems to have lost sight of.

STEVE: Which is?

AQUINAS: We must learn to respect our enemies; first, because the law of Christian charity commands it, but even, considered selfishly, for the very good reason that we can learn much from them.

This obviously does not mean that a man must agree with everything his opponent says, which, in any event, is impossible. What it does mean is that we must not let anger motivate defense of our own views to the point where we lose sight of the wisdom that others can teach us.

I maintain that I was able to sharpen my own intellect, such as it was, by honing it against views that I could not accept.

STEVE: Thank you, Father. Now, Mr. Paine—

PAINE: Before you put questions to me, Mr. Allen, if I may, I should like to address Brother Aquinas directly.

STEVE: (To Aquinas.) Is that all right, Father?

AQUINAS: It is not only all right, Mr. Allen, I'm sure it's inevitable.

PAINE: Very well, Father. Tell me, would you assert that in your voluminous writings you were correct about everything?

AQUINAS: Certainly not, sir.

PAINE: Then if you were not correct about everything, you must have been wrong about some things. And if you were mistaken in any instance, you might be mistaken in any other.

AQUINAS: *(Dryly.)* Yes, Mr. Paine, that would follow. Would you argue that I was mistaken about everything?

PAINE: I would not, sir.

AQUINAS: Then if I were not mistaken in all things, it follows that I must have been right about some. Perhaps it would have behooved you to try to determine those instances in which I was in the right.

ROOSEVELT: Splendid, Father. Can you give us an instance, Mr. Paine, in which St. Thomas was mistaken?

PAINE: I can, indeed sir, and have come prepared to do so. I wonder how many members of the learned doctor's own faith are aware that he disagreed with his predecessor St. Augustine on the subject of *astrology*.

STEVE: In what way?

PAINE: Augustine believed that the stars had influence over nature but denied that they had any effect on human life. Father Aquinas held that stars could actually influence men's bodies and character.

ROOSEVELT: Is this true, Father?

AQUINAS: Yes, it is. I was, however, very careful to preserve the principal of Free Will. The stars do not force man to do anything.

PAINE: In any event, Aquinas, your own church now condemns astrology as gross superstition. You were, therefore, guilty of heresy.

AQUINAS: It is pleasant to hear, Mr. Paine, that you agree with my church about something.

PAINE: In your *Summa Theologica* here, Father, in Volume II, on the subject of the possible existence of planets other than our own Earth, you say, quote, "It is not possible for there to be another Earth than this, because every Earth would naturally be carried to this central one, wherever it was."

Is that a glaring enough error for you, Mr. President?

AQUINAS: I concede the error, Mr. Paine.

PAINE: And in your *Summary Against the Gentiles*, Father, in Book III, on the subject of miracles *(He turns to the proper page)*, you assert that while animals are born according to the biological procedure, even as you and I, you accept the uncommon belief that the low animals, such as insects, can be originated not from their own ancestors but from putrefaction, from waste matter.

Now since such a thing has never happened, sir, you were again in error, were you not?

AQUINAS: I was indeed, Mr. Paine. I always spoke as a theologian, you see, and never made any pretense at special knowledge of the physical sciences. The belief to which you refer was common in my day. You, Mr. Paine, were no doubt a party to certain opinions on scientific questions common in your day that later were shown to be false. We are all, sir, limited by the scientific knowledge available in our times.

ROOSEVELT: Yes, Mr. Paine, a ten-year-old schoolboy today can know more about science than the most learned men of earlier centuries.

PAINE: Of course! But what a pity then that unscientific opinions are not more often advanced with more humility and less an air of certitude.

AQUINAS: I agree. Perhaps, Mr. Paine, my errors under the heading of science were inherent in the nature of that system of thought known as Scholasticism. Being rationalistic it was based therefore upon logic, reason, rather than upon experimental observation or science.

PAINE: I wish to make it clear, however, that there is considerable significance to these errors of fact in the writings of Father Aquinas.

In chapter 103 of the *Summary Against the Gentiles* he says that the eyes of a menstruating woman may affect a mirror.

CLEOPATRA: Now, really.

PAINE: I assert, Your Majesty and gentlemen, that scattered throughout the works of Aquinas there are many such instances of groundless superstition.

Now, that the learned doctor was a gifted practitioner of the art of logic—and a profound and prolific philosopher as well—I would not dream of denying. But when, time and again, he bases his arguments on material things that are supposed to be the case, but which are in reality nonsense, then, it seems to me, we should be on our guard in listening to him.

AQUINAS: You should be on your guard, Mr. Paine, when listening to anyone, including yourself. For even those who intend to speak only the truth will occasionally be mistaken. No one has totally spoken the truth except God.

PAINE: I agree that Almighty God can speak only truth. But you probably refer to the Bible, which because it is full of lies, contradictions, and fairy tales, cannot possibly be the word of an all-good God.

But, my dear sir, it is not enough to say that your errors were only in regard to scientific or technical matters. I can also demonstrate that you were mistaken about what you would call theological or spiritual matters as well.

AQUINAS: Can you indeed?

PAINE: Yes. See here, in paragraph 7, chapter 104 of the *Summary*. You say, and I quote, "The power of self-movement is subsequent to the possession of a soul, for it is proper to animated beings for them to move themselves."

You assert here then, sir, that dogs, cats, cows, lizards, and heaven knows what other creatures all have souls?

AQUINAS: Yes, that is what I wrote. The word animal comes from the Latin word *anima*, meaning spirit.

PAINE: So one understands. But, sir, you have also written that certain Christian beliefs—the Trinity, three persons in one God, and so forth—are incapable of being grasped by the intellect. Yet you also assert your glorious respect for the power of reason.

AQUINAS: That is right, sir.

PAINE: I share your respect for the Goddess Reason, learned doctor, but I do not see how you can accept doctrines that are clearly contrary to the reason you claim to respect!

AQUINAS: You misapprehend me, sir. While affirming that certain doctrines are incapable of being grasped by man's limited intellectual capacities, I deny that these doctrines are contrary to reason. You see, God Himself is a completely rational being, and through his Sacred Scriptures He therefore cannot have taught us anything that would be contrary to His own supreme reason.

But there is no excuse for man to stand mute and helpless before this impenetrable wall. He can leap it with Faith. There is more than enough on his own side of that wall to occupy his time and attention. If a man cannot keep peace in his own house, if he cannot keep the waters of his own soul untroubled, perhaps it does not matter a very great deal that he is unable to measure the mind of God.

CLEOPATRA: Oh, I find all this talk about abstract matters a frightful bore.

Come now, Father, let's talk about more practical things.

STEVE: Such as?

CLEOPATRA: What were your views on womankind?

AQUINAS: *(He laughs.)* Oh, dear me. I am afraid they will find little favor in the present century, Your Majesty. But, like Aristotle, I held that nature, at each birth, always properly wished to produce a male and that therefore when a female was produced, it was a result of something defective or accidental.

CLEOPATRA: *(She gasps in disbelief.)* You don't mean it. No one, Father, neither Aristotle or yourself, has any way of *knowing* what nature "wishes." And if nature got what you imagine to be her wishes, only males would be produced and the human race would shortly disappear.

AQUINAS: I argued that woman contributed only passively to the creation of a new species, although subsequent biological knowledge has, I understand, proved me in error on that specific point.

I argued that woman was the weaker sex, in body, mind, and will.

CLEOPATRA: *(She laughs.)* Preposterous!

AQUINAS: I asserted that the sexual appetite was more predominant in woman than in man.

CLEOPATRA: Oh?

AQUINAS: But of course, as regards either alternative, I could not speak from personal experience.

CLEOPATRA: Didn't it occur to you, Father, that woman and man need each other?

AQUINAS: I wrote that woman needs man in everything, whereas man needs woman only for procreation.

CLEOPATRA: Oh!

AQUINAS: I take it as self-evident that man can accomplish all things better than woman, even those tasks normally considered womanly, such as the care of the home, or cooking, or the making of clothing. Even in these crafts, as I say, the most able practitioners are men.

I also took it as self-evident that woman was unfit to fill any important position, in church or state.

CLEOPATRA: Did you indeed? Then what thought you of all the queens and princesses of antiquity, not to mention your own period of European history?

AQUINAS: In my experience, Your Majesty, queens and princesses reigned in the unhappy absence of kings and princes, and were therefore relatively inferior, even in such high positions.

CLEOPATRA: Insufferable!

AQUINAS: It always seemed reasonable to me that woman should look upon man as her natural master and that she should submit to man's correction and discipline.

CLEOPATRA: Father, what if the woman of a particular pair were intelligent and virtuous, whereas the man was a boor or a fool? What then?

AQUINAS: *(He smiles.)* I wrote, Your Majesty, of things as they should be rather than as they sometimes are.

CLEOPATRA: Ah, hah!

AQUINAS: Again I emphasize that I never claimed infallibility for myself. It belongs only to the Popes. And history has shown that some of my errors and oversights were formidable.

STEVE: Such as?

AQUINAS: Well, I did not foresee, for example, that the Church would one day adopt the doctrine of the Immaculate Conception of the Virgin Mary, which specifies that she was born free from the taint or Original Sin, which stains the souls of all other humans.

PAINE: You also did not anticipate the doctrine of the Infallibility of Popes, Father.

AQUINAS: Quite right.

CLEOPATRA: Well, if you and I have little to agree upon on that ground, Father, perhaps we might see more eye-to-eye in regard to political questions.

AQUINAS: *(He chuckles.)* I am inclined to doubt it, Your Majesty. It was always my view that society and the state exist for the individual, not that the individual exists for the benefit of the state.

CLEOPATRA: You don't mean it!

AQUINAS: You naturally would feel otherwise. And, sad to say, I observe that there are many in the present moment who feel that the rights of the individual are properly subservient to those of the state. Sovereignty, though it comes from God, is vested in the people.

Now, as a practical matter it may be inconvenient for the masses to try to wield power directly. Therefore they generally delegate their sovereignty to some leader or group of overseers.

PAINE: You mean royalty?

AQUINAS: Perhaps, but I could never see the legitimacy of purely heredity rights to the throne, if Your Majesty will forgive me, except in those instances in which such succession was approved by the subject people.

ROOSEVELT: Which would you prefer, Father, a democracy, aristocracy, or monarchy?

AQUINAS: Each can be good, Mr. President, but only if the laws are good and well-administered by wise leadership. Perhaps some form of a constitutional monarchy is best in which, on the one hand, the people are able to depend on the strength of a single wise ruler, but on the other hand a written constitution guarantees the rights of a people, so that, should a leader be tempted to assume more power, the constitution will prevent his doing so.

ROOSEVELT: I must say, Father, that your views are more modern than I might have expected.

AQUINAS: I am not certain, Mr. President, that to be called modern in the present age is entirely a compliment.

ROOSEVELT: What about economics, Father? Did you concern yourself with it?

AQUINAS: Only insofar as it gave rise to moral questions, Mr. President. I did maintain that it is the right of the community—of people through their rulers—to regulate agriculture, industry, or trade for the benefit of the many.

ROOSEVELT: Bully for you!

AQUINAS: I believe it is also morally proper for a community to establish just prices, lest those who have near-total control over goods and services should charge more for them than they are honestly worth.

ROOSEVELT: I am gratified, sir, but greatly surprised. If you were living at the present moment, your views on that particular point would bring you under bitter attack from some quarters.

AQUINAS: *(He laughs.)* Oh, I was quite accustomed to the experience in my own day, I assure you, sir.

PAINE: Tell me, Father, do you favor progressive reform, such as advocated by friend Roosevelt here, or my own more revolutionary ideas?

AQUINAS: Each has its proper place and time, as does the conservative bias, in preserving order and social continuity.

But, Mr. Paine, you and I might both be described as dangerous revolutionaries.

PAINE: Oh?

AQUINAS: In fact, it saddens me that you were never able to perceive the truly revolutionary essence of the Christian message.

PAINE: How's that?

AQUINAS: If I were to ask you who said "*that a small number of very rich men have been able to lay upon the masses of the poor a yoke little better than slavery itself,"* to ask you who might have made such a statement—

ROOSEVELT: Karl Marx or one of the other Socialist philosophers?

AQUINAS: No, sir. The speaker was Pope Leo XIII. And Christ Himself told us that it is easier for a camel to pass through the eye of a needle than it is for a rich man to get into heaven. So, although I concede that the power and authority of the Church have often been misused by the powerful for their own ends, the essential message of Christ is still profoundly revolutionary!

You, Mr. Paine, are considered one of the great dissenters of American and European history. But you are not so great a dissenter, sir, as Jesus Christ.

ROOSEVELT: Well said, Father.

STEVE: Speaking of dissent and revolution, Mr. Paine, there's a question that's puzzled a good many people. The Canadians, the Australians, and others remained happy under the British flag. What caused the Americans to revolt?

PAINE: Oh, many of the problems were economic. You see, the merchants and businessmen who were then becoming so powerful in England did not want competition from merchants and manufacturers in the colonies. In 1750, for example, England passed the Iron Act.

STEVE: Yes, just what was the Iron Act?

PAINE: It prohibited the manufacture of practically all ironware in America. You see, England's economy operated on the mercantile system. Consequently London wanted the colonies to produce raw materials, but to purchase manufactured goods from the mother country.

The British saw themselves as the great storekeepers, and we were supposed to be their willing customers. Ben Franklin warned England of the great folly of such legislation which— though it catered to English business interests—alienated millions in the colonies.

ROOSEVELT: You know, it's odd. If London had listened to the advice of people like Franklin, our country today might still be attached to England.

PAINE: It's quite possible. But at the same time there were many causes for dissatisfaction.

STEVE: Such as?

PAINE: Some of the divisions were along religious lines, providing yet another instance, Father, in which religion has been a destructive rather than beneficial influence.

STEVE: What do you mean?

PAINE: Most English army officers, for example, were strict Anglicans, the Church of England. Consequently they looked down their noses at the peculiar heretics of various kinds they saw in the colonies.

STEVE: Well now, Mr. Paine, before we go much further into the subject of the American Revolution—in which you played so important a role—would you mind if I asked you a few personal questions?

PAINE: I would be disappointed if you did not, sir.

STEVE: You were born in England, weren't you?

PAINE: Yes, in Thetford, Norfolk, in 1737.

STEVE: What did your people do?

PAINE: My father was, by philosophy, a Quaker, by trade a corset maker.

AQUINAS: How were you educated?

PAINE: With great difficulty, sir. For a time I attended the charity school. Since my people were poor, they could afford to give me little formal education.

I began to work as a corset maker at the age of thirteen, for the miserable wages that then prevailed.

STEVE: In what other fields did you work?

PAINE: Oh, I tried my hand as a sailor, a cobbler. I worked for a time as a schoolteacher. I was a tax collector. It was in this last capacity that I became interested in political matters.

STEVE: How did you happen to get to America?

PAINE: I came when I was thirty-eight, in 1774.

STEVE: You mean you got here only two years before the events of 1776?

PAINE: Yes. I had had the extreme good fortune of meeting Benjamin Franklin, to whom not only I but the entire civilized world will always owe a deep debt of gratitude.

ROOSEVELT: Hear, hear!

PAINE: Since I could see little productive future for myself in England, I very much wanted to emigrate to America. Franklin was kind enough to give me a letter of introduction to his son-in-law, Richard Bache, who was helpful in getting me some work as a tutor.

I later had the good fortune to meet a gentleman named Robert Aitken, who planned to publish *The Pennsylvania Magazine*. I talked myself into the job of editor.

STEVE: You'd done a bit of writing in England, hadn't you?

PAINE: Yes, but nothing of mine had ever been published. But when Aitken accepted an article I wrote against slavery, I found the experience of seeing one's words in print rather heady wine.

STEVE: I suppose it doesn't sound very progressive or radical today to be against slavery but two hundred years ago the situation was quite different, wasn't it?

PAINE: Oh, very much so, Mr. Allen. It is extremely important to understand that slavery was not just an offense committed by a few cruel plantation owners or overseers. No, no! Most of the pillars of society of that day were quite prepared to accept slavery. Indeed, a number of my illustrious colleagues of the revolutionary struggle—Washington and Jefferson, to name but two—themselves held slaves on their plantations.

CLEOPATRA: And why not?

PAINE: Because it seemed to me that if the principles of independence and freedom were valid for mankind, then they ought to be applied to the enslaved Negro as well!

By the way, let me ask you something, Mr. Allen. Just before the revolutionary war, what percentage of the population of South Carolina would you say consisted of Negroes?

STEVE: I don't know. Five percent?

PAINE: The answer, sir, is 68 percent!

STEVE: Sixty-eight percent?

PAINE: Yes! More than two-thirds of the people in that state were slaves! In Virginia Negro slaves made up almost half the population.

As regards the treatment accorded those slaves who merely did what any white man would, or ought to, do in the circumstances—which is to say: rise up to free themselves—well, out of deference to Her Majesty and the tender sensibilities of many watching this discussion, I shall not describe the atrocities that were inflicted.

But I do refer you to your libraries, where you may be edified by learning about the slave revolt which took place in 1712 in New York and the similar revolt which occurred in 1741. I will say only that not since the killing of witches in Salem, Massachusetts, had such savagery been perpetrated upon people incapable of defending themselves.

STEVE: Well now, Mr. Paine, there are always a few irresponsible criminals who—

PAINE: Oh, no, sir! I am not talking here about irresponsible acts

committed in a thoughtless moment of passion and later re-
pented of. No, indeed. The atrocities to which I refer were
inflicted by the ruling powers with the full cooperation of the
law, and usually of the Church as well!

AQUINAS: Tragic.

PAINE: Indeed tragic. And you, sir, might be interested to know
the religious affiliations of those who committed such terrible
crimes.

AQUINAS: There is no defense for it, Paine.

CLEOPATRA: Oh, come, come, Mr. Paine, Americans did not invent
slavery. All the nations of my day resorted to it.

PAINE: Indeed, Your Majesty. It is just one more crime for which
mankind must hold royalty responsible.

ROOSEVELT: Was there no kind word said on behalf of the slaves in
the colonies, Mr. Paine.

PAINE: Oh, yes, Mr. Roosevelt. But only by a minority. The only
effective opposition to slavery was made by my father's people,
the Quakers. Oh, the Germans of Pennsylvania were also
helpful. But the Quakers were a century ahead of their time in
this regard, as it seems they often are.

ROOSEVELT: These are painful things to contemplate.

AQUINAS: Yes, Mr. Paine. Are you sure that anything is to be
gained by forcing the people to face such realities?

PAINE: (For a brief moment he is speechless.) Father, you and Mr.
Roosevelt are Christians. I assume, therefore, that you are
guided by the admonition that you shall know the truth and the
truth shall make you free. While I was opposed to organized
religion I never claimed that it was all folly. And one of the wise
precepts of all faiths is that a man's moral condition is utterly
hopeless so long as he believes he is virtuous when in fact he is
not. You cannot possibly be forgiven for a sin if you do not even
admit that you have committed it. The first step toward self-
improvement, therefore, must be to concede that an evil deed
has been done. This is something to be pondered not only by
every man but by every society, for there is none that is without
fault.

STEVE: I understand that among your other advanced ideas, Mr.
Paine, was that of international arbitration.

PAINE: Yes, if I may say so, I was the first to advocate that nations
ought to resort to arbitration just as individuals and other
groups feel obliged to do.

I was also the first to expose the absurdity and criminality of

dueling, a savage and foolish practice. I was the first to suggest
more reasonable ideas of marriage and divorce. And I was the—

CLEOPATRA: Were you ever married yourself, Mr. Paine?

PAINE: Twice, Your Majesty. My first wife died in childbirth, and
from my second I was honorably separated. Divorce, you see,
was in that day impossible under British law.

CLEOPATRA: How quaint.

ROOSEVELT: What did you *think* of marriage, Mr. Paine?

PAINE: Marriage, Mr. President? It is the harbor of human life and
is—with respect to the things in this world—what the next
world is to this. It is *home* and that one word conveys more than
any other word can express.

I understand that presently the American people are much
concerned with the proper care and the rights of animals. Is that
right?

STEVE: Yes.

PAINE: Then you are once more in my debt.

AQUINAS: As you are indebted to your predecessor, St. Francis.

PAINE: *(He smiles.)* Touché, Father.

STEVE: The next thing you'll be telling us is that you were one of
the first spokesmen for women's liberation.

PAINE: *(He reflects briefly.)* I was precisely that, Mr. Allen: the first
in the colonies to demand justice for women. In my day, you
see, women were very definitely second-, if not third-, class
citizens.

AQUINAS: Well, now, there is much to your credit, Mr. Paine, but
just what accounted for your enmity for the churches?

PAINE: Part of my fury at the Church, Father, if I may speak very
frankly, was based on its lamentable failure to practice what it
preached. The two thousand years of Christian history, as you
must know, have been characterized by an enormous amount of
cruelty, bloodshed, terror, despotism, murder, rape, pillage.

AQUINAS: Alas, it is all too true.

PAINE: And, as if that were not bad enough, almost every crime,
almost every atrocity was "justified" by an appeal to a religious
or spiritual cause.

So I felt that the worst fault of the forces of religion was
hypocrisy.

AQUINAS: It is a terrible failing.

PAINE: Oh, there are many evil men. We all do our share of evil, I
suppose. But to do evil while professing virtue is— Well, as I
say, I felt a deep sense of outrage, at the injustices suffered by

many innocent people, and at the use of the Old Testament to justify cruelty of all—

CLEOPATRA: And you no doubt considered yourself virtuous in rebelling against your rightful king?

PAINE: Yes! At first, it may surprise you to learn, Your Majesty, we colonists did not call for rebellion. Many of us hoped, in fact for an honorable reconciliation between England and the American colony-states. But I realized, by the time of the Battle of Lexington, that such hopes were in vain.

ROOSEVELT: With your Quaker background, Paine, and your reputation before the American Revolution as a man of peace, did you find any difficulty in accepting the idea of revolutionary war?

PAINE: I did indeed, Mr. President. The philosophical transition was extremely painful to me. You see, the colonists went through a number of steps: first, resentment at injustice; then, peaceful protest; thirdly, petition for the redress of grievances; later a stage of rebellion; and only at last, very sharply defined revolutionary purpose.

ROOSEVELT: Well, while I certainly disagree with your theological views, you nevertheless merit my respect as one of the leaders of the American Revolution.

PAINE: Thank you, Mr. President.

STEVE: How does the American situation today appear to you, Mr. Paine?

PAINE: (He thinks, briefly.) Well, you don't seem to appreciate what you have, perhaps because you know so little about the tragic suffering of common people in ages past. I think one of the saddest things about this country today is the general lack of interest in history.

CLEOPATRA: Now that is true, Mr. Paine!

PAINE: It is no wonder that so few of you understand what is going on in the present when you have paid so little attention to the past. The past, you see, has created your present, including all the problems that perplex you!

STEVE: Well, if we don't know as much as we should about European history, or ancient history, at least we're pretty well informed about American history, aren't we?

PAINE: Are you serious? There probably isn't a person in your audience who could pass the most elementary examination about the history of this great nation.

But, I repeat, you don't understand revolution today because you don't even understand the American Revolution of two hundred years ago.

STEVE: We don't?

PAINE: No. To be specific: you don't understand what the essence of the Revolution was. Most of you think it was the war with Great Britain. But, as John Adams told us, that was not the essential part of the Revolution. The war was only the effect, the consequence of it. The real revolution was in the minds, the hearts of the people, before a drop of blood had been shed in Lexington.

STEVE: Well, the Americans as a peaceful people do have a—

PAINE: Damn it, sir! You delude yourselves when you tell yourselves that you are a peaceful people! You are not now and never have been, except for a few rare individuals, whom the rest of you often treat quite savagely. But indeed, how could it be otherwise when you are descended from all the savage tribes of Europe, to whom peace has traditionally been only the last resort!

AQUINAS: Agreed, Mr. Paine, for peace generally calls for an exercise of the grand faculties, of compassion, of generosity, of humility, whereas war permits the free flow of all those savage passions from which we derive so much satisfaction!

STEVE: Your Majesty, and gentlemen, we have unfortunately run out of time. Will you all please join us on our next program so we can continue this discussion?

ALL: *(They murmur their agreement.)*

STEVE: Very well. *(He moves away from table as he speaks.)* Those of you who tune in to certain programs hoping to see "big name" guests—well, we hope you've been properly impressed. To keep you happy in that regard we hope, on future programs, to present Sigmund Freud, Sun Yat-sen, Catherine the Great, Abraham Lincoln, Frederick Douglass, and others who, for better or worse, affected history, which is to say, actually had some effect on your life.

There are those who say that the art of conversation is, in our day, dead. If so, we hope to revive it on "Meeting of Minds" by introducing you to others of the important thinkers and doers. And we would be interested to know what you think about what we do here. Thank you and good night.

SHOW #2

President Theodore Roosevelt
(JOSEPH EARLEY)

Queen Cleopatra
(JAYNE MEADOWS)

Father Thomas Aquinas
(PETER BROMILOW)

Thomas Paine
(JOE SIROLA)

&
Steve Allen

STEVE: Welcome once again to "Meeting of Minds." The mind is, among other things, the one attribute of man that marks him as superior to the other animals. One beast or another, you know, is superior to us in one way or another. There are animals that are larger, stronger, fleeter of foot, more beautiful, less warlike. But man alone has a mind that can roam across the vast expanse of time and space. Man alone can make a record of events and ideas and can pass it along to future generations. And yet, an astounding thing has happened. In the present age, when there are so many ways to communicate, we seem to be communicating less effectively than in times past. Social scientists are dismayed to find that even university students cannot read, or write, as well as they should be able to. Which means, I suspect, that they can't think as well as they ought to. It might be helpful to put ourselves into contact with important thinkers, and doers, of times past. Perhaps their experiences, their ideas, their ability to communicate, might stimulate our own thought processes. That, at least, is the rationale for this series of programs.

If you heard the earlier discussion by our four distinguished personages from history, you will already have been informed, stimulated, and perhaps infuriated. I hope so, anyway, because we can easily delude ourselves that having our own prejudices rather neatly arranged in our minds is the same as thinking. It isn't, of course. We're much more likely to learn something when we're challenged.

I can hardly wait to hear what our guests have to say, and it appears that they can hardly wait to question each other.

Good evening, Your Majesty, Mr. President, Gentlemen.

ALL: *(They acknowledge his welcome.)*

ROOSEVELT: I was just about to ask Her Majesty how she met Marc Antony.

CLEOPATRA: Oh, that can wait, Mr. President. I'd rather ask you, How did you develop your dynamic personality?

ROOSEVELT: Well, Your Majesty, I had my father to thank for that. When I was a young boy, I was quite sickly and physically weak. I suffered greatly from asthma, and because of my sickness I couldn't attend school like ordinary children and had to be tutored.

STEVE: You may have been the original ninety-eight-pound weakling.

ROOSEVELT: *(He chuckles.)* Well, my father said to me that if I wanted a strong and healthy body, I would have to make my own. So from that point on, throughout my entire life, I became enthused about athletics: boxing, riding, wrestling, hiking—anything that would build up my body and stamina. When you have a strong, healthy body then you can enjoy life and live every moment of it to the utmost.

STEVE: Speaking of that sort of thing, Mr. President, how did you happen to form the famous "Rough Riders," who fought in the war between Spain and the United States?

ROOSEVELT: The "Rough Riders" were formed by Leonard Wood and myself.

STEVE: Fort Leonard Wood is named after him, isn't it?

ROOSEVELT: Yes, obviously. Anyway the "Rough Riders" were officially called the First Volunteer United States Cavalry. The men were handpicked. They were crack shots, crack riders, with great fighting spirit. They came from all walks of life; polo players from the Main Line in Philadelphia, cowboys from the West, gamblers, poker players—all levels of society—banded together for a common cause.

They were great fighting men, and many of them remained my close friends for the rest of my life.

PAINE: When you were a child, Mr. Roosevelt, did you ever think you would grow up to be president?

ROOSEVELT: Oh, no. When I was a boy I was extremely interested in natural science—wildlife, birds. I even had some of my specimens in the Museum of Natural History in New York when I was only eleven years old!

STEVE: Remarkable.

ROOSEVELT: Yes, I thought so. Anyway, my ambition then was to be a natural scientist. But by the time I got to college I realized that was rather self-limiting, so I switched to law and, after my graduation, I suppose I had a natural affinity for political life because I was elected assemblyman and served in the New York Legislature.

STEVE: But what about Tom Paine's question, Mr. President?

ROOSEVELT: Oh, yes. Well, I suppose I always had an ambition to be president but really never thought about it. I remember one day being visited by my good friend Jacob Riis. There had been some rumor about my running for the presidency! Well, Riis stood in front of my desk and asked me outright, "Do you want to be president?"

I remember saying, "Don't ever ask me that, because if you

ask me, then I have to think about it; and if I think about it, I won't be able to do the job I'm now doing as well as I should; and if I don't do my present job as well as I do, I would never be considered for the presidency!"

STEVE: Mr. President, some historians have said that you acted like an imperialist in the manner in which you achieved the completion of the Panama Canal. Would you agree?

ROOSEVELT: Absolutely not! I simply had the foresight to know that this nation could no longer entertain a policy of isolation! You see, we had come out of the Civil War and had begun to grow and were now ready to take our place among the nations of the world; and if we were to maintain our position, it was of the utmost necessity that we have access to both the Atlantic and Pacific oceans and to the West and the East coasts of this nation.

CLEOPATRA: Mr. President.

ROOSEVELT: Yes?

CLEOPATRA: I see no reason for you to be so defensive on this point. What is wrong with imperialism? There is no real equality in this world—among either men or nations—and it is only common sense that the strong should rule the weak.

ROOSEVELT: I see. Well, Your Majesty, the United States in recent years has not taken quite the same view on that question. In your time might was right; and in later centuries, in Europe, it is true that England, Spain, France, Germany, all carved out enormous territories in other parts of the world. But we Americans do not—

CLEOPATRA: Just a minute, sir! Mr. Paine, did not your country consist first of thirteen small colonies?

PAINE: It did, Your Majesty.

CLEOPATRA: And have I been reliably informed that you have, since that time, by war or other means, taken over territories that belonged to the Indians, to France, to Spain, to Mexico, to Great Britain, to Russia?

ROOSEVELT: Yes, that is true.

CLEOPATRA: And does not the American empire extend this very day to such far-flung outposts as Alaska, the Hawaiian Islands, and Puerto Rico?

ROOSEVELT: Well, yes, but you see, we feel—

CLEOPATRA: Well then I say, bully for you! You've acquired an enormous empire, and you should be proud of it!

ROOSEVELT: But a crucial factor here is that we do not seek domin-
ion over unwilling peoples.

CLEOPATRA: Why not?

AQUINAS: Mr. President, were the American Indians ever *asked* if
they wished to be part of your empire?

ROOSEVELT: Of course not!

CLEOPATRA: And why should they be? My people were proud of
the Egyptian Empire. Gentlemen, my advice to Americans
would be to think of themselves as world-citizens rather than
provincials.

STEVE: How do you mean that, Your Majesty?

CLEOPATRA: Well, the American empire is just about as large as the
old Roman Empire, but you tend to look inward. The Romans,
on the other hand, looked outward, to the whole world.

ROOSEVELT: But, Your Majesty, empire building is not as popular
as it once was.

CLEOPATRA: Oh, come, come, it was probably never popular, Mr.
President. Certainly not with the conquered peoples. But it did
bring civilization to savage and ignorant tribes, did it not?

ROOSEVELT: *(He clears his throat.)* Well . . . to return to the question
of Panama . . . in case of war we had to have fast access to either
ocean, and this could be accomplished only by a pass through
the Isthmus of Panama. In addition, this passage, or canal, had
to be fortified by our nation to prevent, in time of war, access by
enemy fleets. This was the main reason for my insistence upon
the completion of the Panama Canal.

AQUINAS: If you'll permit me, Mr. President, I think Mr. Allen's
original question was a moral one, about the methods of acquir-
ing control in Panama.

ROOSEVELT: Well, Father, there are many stories about how this
was accomplished. I would like to give you the facts. We had
originally negotiated, but had not ratified, a treaty with Colombia, which at that time was occupying Panama without the
consent of the people of Panama. Now if the Latin Americans
want to talk about imperialism and conquest let them talk about
their attacks upon each other!

Anyway, this treaty called for the use of the land for building
a canal, in exchange for ten million dollars, plus two hundred
and fifty thousand dollars annually, for the next nine years.

Now the Colombians did not ratify this treaty, as they
thought they could get more money from us, or more money

from the French, who had the French-Panama Company there, at that time. In any event, we had five choices.

STEVE: What were they?

ROOSEVELT:

1. I could pay more money to Colombia, but I had a great distaste for blackmail.
2. I could delay the canal until a new agreement was made with Colombia.
3. I could abandon Panama for Nicaragua, but studies showed that Panama was the better site.
4. I could occupy the Canal Zone by force.
5. I could await *revolution* in Panama.

STEVE: Which of the five did you choose?

ROOSEVELT: I chose this last option because of information given to me by a Mr. Bunau-Varilla, an engineer with the French-Panama Company. He told me that the people of Panama were on the verge of revolution against the Colombian repression, and that it would only be a matter of days!

Now, if this revolt were successful, I saw the answer to my problem, which would be to recognize the Republic of Panama and negotiate a treaty with them for the use of what would be the Canal Zone. Well, by George, the revolution did take place, but I gave no aid whatsoever to the revolutionaries.

STEVE: You did send gunboats down there, didn't you?

ROOSEVELT: Yes, but that was to protect American nationals and to prevent Colombian troops from landing.

STEVE: Mr. President, you also had the reputation of being against Big Business.

ROOSEVELT: *(Angrily.)* Poppycock! I was not against Big Business! But I was against its abuse by selfish individuals.

AQUINAS: Are you talking about moral offenses?

ROOSEVELT: Absolutely! There was a definite need for a regulation of giant corporations by the government, in the interest of the public. You and I have to obey the laws. Why should Big Business be an exception? A corporation should have such regulation over it as to guarantee that its activity shall be exercised only in ways beneficial to the public. To prevent abuses, the regulation of corporations is no more a move against liberty than putting a stop to violence or crime is a move against liberty.

Of course, this regulation should take place under the leadership of responsible men anxious to conserve the just rights of property. But, at the same time, human rights must be paramount in a republic such as ours.

Power over corporations must be exercised, for unless they are controlled by the government they will, themselves, completely control government!

STEVE: That sounds very much like President Eisenhower's warning about the "military-industrial complex."

ROOSEVELT: Is that right?

But now, Mr. Allen, I must insist. Her Majesty promised earlier to tell me about her . . . er . . . relationship with Marc Antony.

STEVE: Very well.

Would you have any objection to hearing the details, Father?

AQUINAS: Not at all, sir. Her Majesty died just a few years before she could have heard the message of Christ, and even the Old Testament was unknown to her. We cannot, therefore, hold her to account on standards concerning which she knew nothing.

PAINE: And remember, Aquinas, her conduct was no worse than that of generations of Christian kings and queens who gave lip service to your code but were apparently rarely guided by it in their personal lives.

STEVE: Very well, Your Majesty, how did Marc Antony come into your life?

CLEOPATRA: Well, I first met him when I was quite young, while living in Rome with Caesar. But when Caesar died there was a terrible struggle for power. One group was led by the young man Octavian, who was Caesar's grandnephew and legal heir. Marc Antony led the other. He was a powerful general, and when he saw that Octavian was only a boy, and an invalid at that, he declined to give up the power he had taken upon himself.

ROOSEVELT: What sort of a fellow was Marc Antony?

CLEOPATRA: *(She smiles, thinking back.)* Hah! He was, as you might say, really something. Big, handsome, like a Hercules. When he came to meet me in Tarsus—

AQUINAS: Ah, yes, Tarsus. The home of St. Paul.

CLEOPATRA: *(She ignores the interruption.)* When he came to meet me, I arrived on my most luxurious Egyptian galley. It had purple sails and oars of silver. Antony had sent an ambassador to

Egypt inviting me to meet him in Tarsus. Well, I met him, and— *(She chuckles.)*

ROOSEVELT: And, to paraphrase Caesar, you came, you saw, you conquered.

STEVE: Was it purely a matter of love on your part?

CLEOPATRA: He, shall we say, forgot about his military campaigns and decided to spend the winter in Alexandria with me.

ROOSEVELT: What was Alexandria like in those days, Your Majesty?

CLEOPATRA: To me it was the most exciting city in the ancient world. It was like your Paris, New York, Venice, Rome, San Francisco, all rolled into one.

But the following spring Antony had to return to his duties. It was four long years before I saw him again. It was four years, too, before he saw the twins.

STEVE: Twins?

CLEOPATRA: Yes. The baby boy and girl that I gave him. We named the boy Alexander, for the sun, and the girl Cleopatra, for the moon.

STEVE: And you were Antony's last wife?

CLEOPATRA: Oh, no. He later married the sister of Octavian, my enemy. Her name was Octavia.

STEVE: Did that make you jealous?

CLEOPATRA: Not at all. Their marriage was largely a matter of political convenience. Though he married Octavia, I was still the one he loved. When, after four years, Antony returned to me, he told me he planned to conquer Parthia. I was glad to furnish gold and supplies. I went with him as far as the Euphrates River to see him off.

ROOSEVELT: That military campaign turned out to be a disaster, didn't it?

CLEOPATRA: Yes. Things went from bad to worse. Antony was furious because Octavian had attacked me. So he sent a bill of divorcement to his wife. That lost him many friends in Rome. Octavian talked the Roman Senate into declaring war on me.

STEVE: What did Antony do about that?

CLEOPATRA: He had no recourse but to defend me against the forces of Rome. It was to be our undoing. When disaster followed upon disaster Antony misunderstood a message that I was thinking of killing myself. He thought I had already done so, and plunged a sword into his own side. When he regained consciousness and learned that I was still alive, he begged to be carried to me. His stretcher had to be lifted up the front of the mausoleum wall behind which I was protected. A few minutes later—he died in my arms.

Octavian entered the city and captured it. He promised to treat me honorably, but I knew he was lying. I learned that he was secretly planning to take me back to Rome and display me as a captive! I would have none of it. I begged permission to visit Antony's tomb and bent down and kissed the cold marble that covered him. I wept for hours at his loss.

I then dressed myself in my most beautiful gown; put on these jewels that you so admired, sir; ordered my quarters to be prepared, as if for a feast; and, with a small poisonous snake, ended my life.

STEVE: What happened to your children?

CLEOPATRA: My children by Antony were spared. They were taken to Rome and made welcome by Antony's former wife, Octavia.

STEVE: If you had been in her place, Your Majesty, would you have been noble enough to do the same?

CLEOPATRA: (She pauses, thinking back.) Absolutely not!

ROOSEVELT: What about Caesarion, Little Caesar, your son by Julius Caesar?

CLEOPATRA: He was—executed, Mr. President. It was a great tragedy which my own death spared my witnessing. Think of it. That child was the last of the Ptolemy rulers of Egypt, and the only son that Julius Caesar ever had. But Octavian had at last triumphed and ruled Rome alone, as Augustus Caesar.

STEVE: Thank you, Your Majesty.

Now, Mr. Paine, during your earlier visit here, sir, you were telling us about the causes that led to the American Revolution.

PAINE: Yes. Well, part of the problem was simply a battle over land speculation, the same sort of thing that is not unknown to you people here in California.

STEVE: Would you explain that?

PAINE: Well, you see, after France was defeated on the North American Continent, this left her Indian allies—such as the Ottawa Tribe, led by Chief Pontiac—at the mercy of the British colonists, who began to encroach on the Indians' territories.

STEVE: About when was that?

PAINE: Well, in 1763 Pontiac organized a counterattack. This may surprise you, but some of the colonists did not even rise to their own defense but left it to the King's royal troops to put down the Indian uprising.

ROOSEVELT: Also, Mr. Paine, I understand that the British were eager to keep the loyalty of the former French citizens in the colony of Quebec, as a counterweight to the rebelliousness that was beginning to grow in other colonies.

PAINE: You're quite right, Mr. Roosevelt. To prevent any further such trouble, as he thought, anyway, George III issued his royal proclamation of October 1763.

STEVE: What did he proclaim?

PAINE: That there would be no further purchases or settlement by the colonists in that region between the Allegheny Mountains and the Mississippi, from Quebec all the way down to Florida.

ROOSEVELT: Did the colonists abide by the proclamation?

PAINE: They did not, Mr. President. On the contrary, a great army of over thirty thousand settlers crossed the mountains and took such land as they could hold. In fact, a number of my colleagues, Washington, Ben Franklin, and Patrick Henry organized land companies.

STEVE: Land companies?

PAINE: Yes, to sell land to the newcomers. So you see, right from the start Americans have been specialists in the real estate business.

Things went from bad to worse when in 1774 the British Parliament passed what was called the Quebec Act. This act stipulated that the entire territory north of the Ohio River be annexed to the old province of Quebec. This was supposed to put an end to the squabbling between Pennsylvania, Virginia, and other colonies over the land in question.

STEVE: Did it?

PAINE: Not at all. In fact, partly out of anger at the Quebec Act, Virginia issued the call to the First Continental Congress, which took place in Philadelphia in 1774, as you might recall.

STEVE: Was that congress called specifically to discuss rebellion?

PAINE: No. It was motivated largely by love of liberty and by exasperation with the increasing shortsightedness of George III and his Parliament.

STEVE: I see. Wasn't taxation also an important issue?

PAINE: Indeed yes. The Seven Years War against France and Austria had been very costly to England, and the expense of administering the new American empire was enormous. To help defray these costs, the British introduced a series of levies and duties— on paper, on tea, on lead, on sugar— on all sorts of things. We did not take very kindly to these tactics, and we hated even more the snooping customs agents, who became completely intolerable in their attempts to ensure collection.

STEVE: I see. Just when did violence first break out?

PAINE: That would be in 1768 when an American mob attacked British customs agents who were trying to collect duties from John Hancock's ship, the *Liberty*. The rioting naturally made the British bring in more troops. There was a great deal of talk about law and order at that time, as I recall.

For about a year and a half an uneasy peace was maintained in the area. Then, in March 1770, some Americans threw just snowballs at the British redcoats whose officers responded with an order to fire on the attackers.

CLEOPATRA: Good.

PAINE: It was not good, Your Majesty. Four Bostonians were killed.

There was no further open rebellion until 1773 which, you may recall, is the year that the Boston Tea Party took place.

STEVE: Yes. What was the Boston Tea Party all about anyway?

PAINE: It was chiefly a business dispute, Mr. Allen. You see, the British Parliament had given the East India Company a monopoly on the tea trade in America. Naturally American tea merchants were not very happy about this. The company didn't even employ local sales agents, so the Americans were deprived even of sales commissions. So—the East India Company's tea was dumped into Boston harbor.

Fortunately—from the point of view of us revolutionaries— the British Parliament again overreacted. They passed what were called the Coercive Acts. We called them the Intolerable Acts. The measures ordered the closing of the Port of Boston, the quartering of British troops in American colonists' homes, and the shipment of the worst offenders to England for trial.

CLEOPATRA: I should think so!

PAINE: Hearing of the growing troubles, the British appointed General Gage as Governor of Massachusetts. He quartered his troops in Boston. It was then that John Hancock and others began to organize resistance. Munitions dumps were established outside of Boston.

STEVE: How did General Gage react to that?

PAINE: He sent a detachment to confiscate the arms. On April 18, 1775, Paul Revere learned of the approach of the British and roused the Minutemen to stand against the invaders at Lexington. Eight Americans were killed, and the British proceeded on to Concord where the "embattled farmers," as you've been told, "fired the shot heard round the world."

STEVE: Did the colonists unite in a great patriotic fervor once the war had started?

PAINE: *(He laughs.)* Mr. Allen, as to whether we were patriots depends upon one's point of view. In a sense, the American rebels were not patriots at all. We were the traitors, the revolutionaries, the subversives. We were the rebels against the mother country. Those who remained loyal to England considered themselves patriots. But your question dealt with unity. Good God, no, there couldn't possibly have been unity since there were so many different points of view among the colonists.

STEVE: Really?

PAINE: Yes. Those who remained loyal to the King and the English Church numbered in the hundreds of thousands. You see, as the long quarrel between the colonies and England developed, two distinct parties emerged.

STEVE: What were they?

PAINE: One consisted of the radicals. It was the radicals who were strongly opposed to the British government. The other group was the conservatives.

STEVE: I see. Just who were the radicals?

PAINE: They consisted mainly of lower- and middle-class people, while the conservatives were mostly wealthy and educated, some of them aristocrats. You see, even if England had disappeared overnight in a puff of smoke, many of the aristocrats of America would still have been opposed to the common people, who were beginning to rise up. The leaders of the colony of Georgia, for example, were much more in favor of England and had very little interest in revolution. In fact, Georgia did not even send representatives to the First Continental Congress.

STEVE: Is that right?

PAINE: Yes. But fortunately for the revolution, the Sons of Liberty—Samuel Adams, myself, and other "troublemakers"—managed, shall we say, to intimidate those who were less outspoken.

But you must understand that at that time revolutionary
sentiment was felt by only about a third of the people in
America. Another third, more or less, were opposed to revolution, and the remaining third consisted of people who, I suppose, didn't want to get involved.

STEVE: Yes, we still have them with us.

AQUINAS: They exist in every age.

PAINE: Because of this we might never have achieved independence
were it not for the folly of the British Parliament in over-
responding to the situation. Naturally, the more stupid and
aggressive the British became, the more force they employed,
the more these moves angered the colonists, and therefore
tended to unite them.

STEVE: I see. But I return to my earlier question. Once hostilities
had broken out, was it all a noble campaign from that point on?

PAINE: (He looks shocked.) I am appalled, sir, that you modern Americans know so little of war, particularly when you have had such
experience with it.

AQUINAS: Yes, it is possible that noble considerations may lead to
war, but once a war starts nobility of motive finds itself allied
with expediency, which will in turn enlist almost any vice to
attain its end.

PAINE: You are quite right, Father. But the idea that the American
colonists were almost totally heroic is utterly without founda-
tion. Most of the colonists, frankly, had very little enthusiasm
for war when they realized that British manpower was about
five times as great as that of the thirteen colonies, and that the
ships of the British Navy outnumbered ours by one hundred
to one!

STEVE: One hundred to one? Amazing.

PAINE: England was the richest country in the world at the time,
and the colonies were not a nation at all. Nor were our fighting
forces really prepared for war.

STEVE: Well, don't these very facts suggest that the American
colonists must have been heroic fighters to overcome such
odds?

PAINE: Only a relatively small number, sir. As I look back now, I
realize that we quite possibly would have lost the revolutionary
war had it not been that Spain, France, and Holland eventually
declared war against Great Britain and came in on our side.

STEVE: That was no doubt a help, but what about our great hero
George Washington?

PAINE: Well, Washington was a great man, and a fine general, though he did make a few mistakes; and I personally had my disagreements with him in the long run. We had several good commanders, as well as a small and courageous professional army. But the majority of the American fighting forces were untrained, undisciplined, and as often cowardly as not.

ROOSEVELT: Cowardly?

PAINE: Yes! This was one of the most important reasons, you see, why I had to criticize "the summer soldiers and the sunshine patriots"!

The members of the militia and the volunteers had very little interest in fighting. They knew the wages were poor; the equipment was, for the most part, disgraceful; the hospital services were almost nonexistent; while the British troops, on the other hand, were disciplined professionals.

ROOSEVELT: Well, our men did enlist!

PAINE: Yes, but only for short periods of time, and in many cases they would not remain in the army so much as an extra ten minutes once their terms had expired. Some even left their posts in the middle of battle!

ROOSEVELT: Well, at least the officers were a courageous and disciplined bunch because after all the—

PAINE: Mr. Roosevelt, you surprise me. I would think that you would be aware that in speaking of his officers, in 1776, George Washington said that "except in a few instances they are not worth the bread they eat!"

STEVE: You know, it's interesting, Mr. Paine, that those Americans today who can trace their ancestry back to revolutionary times feel very proud if they can claim an ancestor who was simply alive at the time of the revolutionary war.

PAINE: Really?

CLEOPATRA: Oh, how amusing.

PAINE: But, I repeat, the heroes on our side were very few, relatively speaking. Fortunately, in the long run, the few heroic officers and men greatly distinguished themselves. The British made many mistakes, and their task was extremely difficult anyway in that they were trying to fight a war many thousands of miles away from their homeland, a difficulty with which I understand Americans have in recent years had some experience.

STEVE: Then perhaps one reason the Americans finally won out is that they were fighting in their homeland, where the local villagers and townspeople were glad to help them.

PAINE: That was by no means always the case. You know today, of course, of the tragic sufferings of Washington's army during the winter of 1777–1778 at Valley Forge. But apparently most Americans know little more of that story than they might learn from looking at a painting of Washington and his troops in the snow. It was, after all, snowing all throughout that area. Therefore the question arises why only Washington's troops were suffering.

STEVE: I don't know. Why was that?

PAINE: There were a number of reasons, one of which was the stupidity and weakness of Congress in neglecting to provide for the material needs of the soldiers. Another factor was the selfishness of the Pennsylvania farmers who refused to sell food to Washington's soldiers because all they had was paper money. Instead they sold it to the British troops because from them they received payment in good English gold.

ROOSEVELT: Disgraceful!

STEVE: Well, perhaps, Mr. Paine, you're describing just isolated incidents, or a state of affairs that lasted for a very short time.

PAINE: Not at all, Mr. Allen. As late as 1780 Washington's soldiers were still without adequate food and clothing and partly as a result were not only deserting but were in many cases even going over to the enemy!

STEVE: Incredible. To the enemy?

PAINE: Yes, it was about this time, by the way, that the treason of Benedict Arnold was discovered. Now perhaps you can see why I was driven to write my "Crisis" papers.

STEVE: Yes. I never completely understood it before!

PAINE: It was terribly necessary to do something dramatic to keep up the fighting spirit of the colonists! I felt it was necessary constantly to remind the colonists what they were fighting for, to remind them of ideas such as those contained in Jefferson's Declaration of Independence.

CLEOPATRA: A most impudent document.

STEVE: To the extent, Your Majesty, that you frown upon ideas such as those found in the French Rights of Man, the American Bill of Rights, and the Declaration of Independence, you may be gratified to learn that the freedoms those documents guaranteed are apparently less popular today than they were two hundred years ago!

CLEOPATRA: And with good reason. Your "glorious" freedom was an absurd experiment from the first, a passing phase.

PAINE: You Americans today take a rather narrow view of the Declaration, it seems to me. You see it in terms of vaguely admirable sentiments, and the wording sounds to you rather like the wording of a prayer that you mouth without thinking of its meaning. But the *real* underlying historic significance of the Declaration was that it expressed a growing attitude by thoughtful men in many parts of the planet, a growing questioning of the divinity of kings . . . and queens. It was written at a time, you see, when divinity itself was coming seriously into question.

AQUINAS: *(He looks sharply at Paine.)*

PAINE: If there were no divine daily personal ruler of the whole universe, it followed that human kings could not possibly be in any sense divine, nor could it be said that their right to rule came from a supreme being.

CLEOPATRA: *(She slaps the table angrily.)* Mr. Paine, even if there were no gods, we queens, kings, and emperors have a right to rule simply because we are superior! It is only common sense that the intelligent should rule the ignorant, that the strong should rule the weak.

PAINE: Since many of the crowned heads of Europe were, and had been for centuries, personally monstrous—

CLEOPATRA: Some of them.

PAINE: Many of them! We were saying then, in a word, to hell with kings!
(*He addresses the audience.*) Keep that in mind now as you rethink these words: We hold these truths to be self-evident, that all men are created equal—

CLEOPATRA: They most certainly are not!

AQUINAS: Her Majesty is correct, in one sense. Nature itself exists in the form of a hierarchy, which means that all things are not equal. Some occupy positions of higher importance, others are inferior. As for the human race, it is obvious that no two men, or women, are precisely equal in strength, in beauty, in intelligence. There are many natural differences.

CLEOPATRA: Precisely.

AQUINAS: But all men are of equal importance in the sight of God, Your Majesty, and therefore must be equal before the law!

PAINE: Thank you, Father. That they are endowed by their Creator with certain inalienable rights, that among these are life, liberty, and the pursuit of happiness—that to secure these rights governments are instituted among men, deriving their just powers from the consent of the governed.

CLEOPATRA: The shepherd, Mr. Paine, has never sought the consent of the sheep!

PAINE: Shepherds, Your Majesty, in the long run rob the sheep of their wool, kill them, and *eat* them!

To continue—that whenever any form of government becomes destructive of these ends, it is the right of the people to alter or abolish it and to institute new government!

CLEOPATRA: What a pity, Mr. Paine, that your fine, flowery words are motivated chiefly by the contempt in which you evidently hold royalty.

PAINE: You misunderstand my views, Your Majesty. I am not the personal enemy of kings . . . or queens, particularly one so attractive as yourself. Quite the contrary. No man wishes more heartily than myself to see them all in a happy and honorable state, as private individuals. But I am the avowed, open, and intrepid enemy of the institution of the monarchy. It is against the hell of monarchy that I declared eternal war!

I wish you personally, Your Majesty, the very best of good fortune.

ROOSEVELT: What would have happened to Mr. Paine in your time, Your Majesty, if he had written or made such statements?

CLEOPATRA: Executed! He would have been beheaded, Mr. President. Heresy and treason were never tolerated in my time, nor should they ever be! Instant apprehension and execution saved a great deal of time and energy and useless debate, such as this. It also helped to preserve and perpetuate the state. The Egyptian Empire did not last for so many thousands of years by tolerating troublemakers!

ROOSEVELT: Do you deny, Your Majesty, that common citizens have any rights?

CLEOPATRA: They have such "rights," sir, as wise rulers may choose to grant them!

AQUINAS: If all rulers were wise, Your Majesty, there would be no need for revolution.

PAINE: Well said, Aquinas!

CLEOPATRA: Outrageous! *(She stands, furious.)*

Look about you in the world, Mr. Paine, and see what your fine rhetoric about revolution has produced! Do you see universal peace? Do you see universal order? Do you see widespread respect for the basic virtues? Now, that there have been despots among the monarchy down through the centuries is quite clear enough, but I do not see that *uninformed mobs*—called the *majorities*, if you will—are any the better.

PAINE: Your prejudices are quite understandable, Your Majesty, given the nature of your personal experience. A queen naturally feels that she is entitled to her high estate.

STEVE: *(Attempting to make peace.)* Well . . . to get back to your experiences during the revolutionary war, Mr. Paine—

PAINE: Yes. Since I counted myself a man of action, in 1776 I resigned from the magazine I'd been working for and joined the army, as what you might call a propaganda specialist. I marched with Washington and his troops.

AQUINAS: Were the American forces victorious from the start?

PAINE: Quite the contrary, Father; the war dragged on for seven agonizing years, and much of the time there was suffering, defeat, and humiliation. At one point an army of twenty thousand had withered away to just a few hundred beaten and hopeless men. By December 1776 all seemed lost. It was as a result of these sufferings that I wrote the following lines, which some of you may remember:

> These are the times that try men's souls. The summer soldier and the sunshine patriot will, in this crisis, shrink from the service of his country; but he that stands with it now deserves the love and thanks of man and woman. Tyranny, like hell, is not easily conquered. Yet we have this consolation with us, that the harder the conflict, the more glorious the triumph. What we obtain too cheap we esteem too lightly!

ROOSEVELT: What was the effect of these words?

PAINE: I will not be falsely modest, sir. There was no other single factor which so electrified and revived the sagging spirits of the American Army. The words were from a paper called "Crisis." It was read in the army camps. Speakers repeated my words. The results were so beneficial that during the war I wrote a total of thirteen "Crisis" papers, one for each colony.

STEVE: Was there any one military confrontation, Mr. Paine, that might be described as a turning point for the colonial forces?

PAINE: Yes, I suppose the Battle of Saratoga could be so described. We colonists had at that point been fighting for over two years, without much success. The British soldiers, as I've already told you, were *far* superior to our own. *Our* men, you see, were not very well trained, and they consisted for the most part of militia rather than regular army. But at Saratoga, New York, the accidents of nature conspired to give the Americans a victory.

STEVE: How did that happen, sir?

PAINE: Well, you see, British General John Burgoyne was moving down from Canada in an attempt to drive a wedge between the New England area and the other colonies. He was doing quite well until he reached the Saratoga area, a section of mostly dense forest. Because of the trees and other natural cover the terrain was not ideally suited to the open-field tactics that the British, and other European armies, were accustomed to.

But the seven thousand colonists in the area, under such leaders as Daniel Morgan and Benedict Arnold, naturally protected themselves by hiding behind trees, bushes, and rocks.

Another factor was that the British wore uniforms of a brilliant red color, and this made firing upon them relatively easy, whereas our forces were not so colorfully attired.

STEVE: Were the British headed toward certain defeat from that point on?

PAINE: Oh, by no means. The war continued for several more years, but the stunning American victory in Saratoga did show European observers of the war that the British could be defeated; and it was this battle, in my view, that chiefly induced the French to finally come in on our side.

CLEOPATRA: I suppose the writing of your patriotic books and pamphlets made you a rich man, did it, Mr. Paine?

PAINE: On the contrary, Your Majesty. I was never anything but poor. For a time my income from Congress was a mere seventy dollars a month, on which I could barely live. I refused, during the battle, to accept royalties from my patriotic writings. It was not until 1780, at which time I began to think of writing a history of the Revolution, that I felt justified in seeking monetary return from my writings.

STEVE: You didn't spend the rest of your life in the United States, did you?

PAINE: I did not, sir. In 1787 I went to Europe, intending to stay for a year. I wished to see my parents, who were then still alive in Britain. I also wished to revisit France, but . . . time has a way of surprising us. It was to be fifteen long years before I returned to American shores.

STEVE: What kept you there so long?

PAINE: Well, for one thing I shortly found myself in the middle of the French Revolution.

STEVE: *(With a laugh.)* You just couldn't stay out of trouble.

PAINE: Excuse me. Might I have something to drink?

STEVE: Yes, of course. *(He pours.)*

PAINE: In recognition of my efforts Lafayette personally gave me the enormous key to the Bastille prison, which I transmitted to George Washington. *(He drinks.)* Why, this is *water*!

STEVE: Ah, then the stories of you that you were a bit of a drinker are true?

PAINE: Sir, I lived in an age when heavy drinking was common. In that time I was considered a moderate drinker. I was never an alcoholic, as some of my critics have alleged.

ROOSEVELT: You ought to have taken better care of your health, sir. You had ought not to have drunk at all.

STEVE: Pardon me, Mr. President. How old were you when you died?

ROOSEVELT: I was sixty-one years old.

STEVE: I see. Well, Mr. Paine lived to be seventy-two.

ROOSEVELT: But to get back to the French Revolution. You don't approve of everything done in its name, do you?

PAINE: Obviously not, Mr. President, since I ended up in a French prison cell myself. The men I called my friends in the French Revolution were eventually defeated. Then came the reign of terror, the execution of the King, of Queen Marie Antoinette, and more. All of this saddened me greatly. It might interest you to know, Your Majesty, that I tried to prevent the execution of the King.

CLEOPATRA: *(Coldly.)* Did you?

PAINE: Yes. One of the saddest things about man is that he is so easily disposed to execute those of whom he disapproves.

STEVE: Well, now everything we've learned about you so far, Mr. Paine, seems eminently admirable. You are obviously one of the heroes of the American Revolution, and your general good sense is clear. Why then would President Roosevelt and others be so critical of you in after years?

ROOSEVELT: That was for another of his books, Mr. Allen. It was called *The Age of Reason*. What a pity he wrote it!

PAINE: Did you ever read it, sir?

ROOSEVELT: Er . . . well, no . . . but I read commentaries on it.

PAINE: It is still being published. Let men read it and make up their own minds.

It might interest you to know, Mr. President, that I wrote a bit of it in Luxembourg prison, while expecting to be executed. I was at the time reviled in my native land, England, largely neglected by George Washington and the American government. I was imprisoned by the French, and in such a predicament a man might easily succumb to despair, perhaps even to suicide. Instead I began to plan *The Age of Reason*, to contemplate the power, the wisdom, and the goodness of God in His works.

AQUINAS: One is pleased to know you finally found time for such a pursuit, Mr. Paine.

PAINE: *(Ignoring the thrust.)* In 1794 when the Terror began to abate, I was released from prison. I had spent almost a year behind bars. After my release I finished *The Age of Reason.*

ROOSEVELT: Since you are not an atheist, sir, precisely what was your religion?

PAINE: It was the religion called Deism, Mr. Roosevelt, the worship of the God revealed in the heavens and in his works in nature. I believed there should be no middleman between a man and his God.

AQUINAS: What obligations did your faith place upon you, Mr. Paine?

PAINE: *(He chuckles.)* What a remarkably Catholic question, Father. Under the God of Deism I felt that my religious duties consisted in doing justice, loving mercy, and endeavoring to make one's fellow creatures happy.

ROOSEVELT: It sounds all too easy.

PAINE: Mr. President, for your information my faith was substantially shared by such American heroes as Benjamin Franklin, John Adams, Thomas Jefferson, George Washington, and many outstanding men of the time, and not only in the United States but in Great Britain and France as well! It was an important part of the larger philosophical movement called the Enlightenment, in which the wisest men were beginning to turn their backs on superstition and cruelty.

ROOSEVELT: Yes, yes, we've heard all that. But why didn't Washington and Jefferson and the rest get into the same kind of trouble you did if they shared some of your views on religious matters?

PAINE: *(He smiles.)* Well, sir, most of them followed Franklin's advice not to spit in the wind lest it blow back in their faces. I do not criticize my colleagues, but I felt that I had to speak out, rather than hide my true beliefs. I believed that all national institutions of churches—whether Jewish, Christian, Turkish, or whatever—were no more than human inventions, set up largely to terrify and enslave men and to assist in the monopolization of power and profit! Since you have raised the question, sir, I quote directly from *The Age of Reason (He opens the book.):*

> I do not mean by this declaration to condemn those who believe otherwise; they have the same right to their belief as I have to mine. But it is necessary to the happiness of man, that he be mentally faithful to himself. Infidelity does not consist in believing, or in disbelieving; it consists in professing to believe what he does *not* believe.

AQUINAS: It must come as a great surprise to you now, Mr. Paine, to know that the chief victim of your attacks upon the Scriptures was a certain rigid form of literalist fundamentalism, and that today a good many of your criticisms of Scripture are accepted by millions of devout Christians.

PAINE: *(He smiles.)* I concede that I would not have anticipated that result, Father. But to the extent that Christian belief has evolved and become more civilized in the last two hundred years, I naturally approve of the changes that have taken place.

AQUINAS: My own view, Mr. Paine, concerning your criticisms of the follies and crimes committed by Christians, and other believers, down through the centuries, is that you have spoken much truth; but you have by no means given a balanced picture. If the Churches were truly as evil and misguided as you say, they would not have persisted so long, nor would you find so many millions of people certain that they have derived deep comfort, and that their emotional needs have been met, by their religious faith.

It seems to me that your rightful claim to fame is in your capacity as author of *Common Sense* and *The Rights of Man* rather than *The Age of Reason.*

CLEOPATRA: How was your life ended, Mr. Paine?

PAINE: I spent the last few years of my life, Your Majesty, in a miserable rooming house at 309 Bleecker Street in New York City. I lived on the second floor.

In 1809 I was moved, as an invalid, to 50 Grove Street and died there shortly thereafter.

ROOSEVELT: Did you change any of your religious views on your deathbed?

PAINE: I consider the question insulting, Mr. President, although I'm sure that was not your intention.

ROOSEVELT: Oh, are you?

PAINE: In my last months I was troubled by a number of fanatics who forced their way into my quarters and attempted to get me to recant before, as they supposed, I should suffer the tortures of the damned. I remember a peculiar woman came to me, purporting to bring a personal message from God. I said to her, "My good woman, you were not sent with such a pertinent message . . . God would not in any event send such a foolish, ugly old woman as *you* with His messages. Go away and shut the door behind you!"

AQUINAS: You seem very proud of your accomplishments and very certain in your views, Mr. Paine. Is there nothing you regret about what you did or wrote?

PAINE: Oh, of course. All of us have our regrets and sorrows, Father. I regret that I was not, like yourself, a saintly person. I lived an essentially decent life, I suppose, but I always found it easier to love mankind than individual human beings.

AQUINAS: *(He smiles.)* All of us have suffered from that difficulty, Mr. Paine, and perhaps the saints most of all.

PAINE: I regret, too, that I was not able to be more charitable with the many who attacked me. I would say my greatest failing was my inability to compromise. But . . . *(he shrugs)* probably if I had it to do all over again, I would behave the same. For certainly you must know that few men have ever been so viciously and unfairly attacked, and that sir, chiefly by people who considered themselves Christians!

Any vicious abuse, any lie, any slander, was considered permissible as long as Thomas Paine was the target of it.

I was alleged to be a drunkard, an adulterer, a traitor, an atheist. Every one of those charges was false.

Tell me, Aquinas, what significance do you attach to the nature of the attacks upon me?

AQUINAS: *(He thinks briefly.)* It seems to me, Mr. Paine, that your most violent critics were probably those least certain of their own faith. Because their faith was lightly held, although they might not have realized it, you startled them in jarring their smug assumptions. This sent them into a great state of alarm and fear. It was their fear, I would think, that created their hostility.

ROOSEVELT: Father Aquinas, you dealt with a great many heretics and unbelievers in your day. Were you always so kindly disposed to them as you think Paine's critics ought to have been to him?

AQUINAS: *(He laughs heartily.)* A marvelous question, Mr. Roosevelt! The answer is, no. I confess I was sometimes driven to anger and deep resentment at what I regarded as the dangerous heresies of some of my adversaries. But I did attempt to counter their arguments in the spirit of Christian charity, and in my writings I think I was largely successful in this endeavor.

ROOSEVELT: Yes, Aquinas, I believe you were.

PAINE: My friends, we come now to a most interesting point, and we should pause to consider it most carefully. Her Majesty has already been frank enough to tell us that had I broadcast my views in her time she would have put me to death! No doubt most painfully. The rest of us here at this table—now think this through very carefully—the rest of us would seem to consider her intended conduct morally abominable. It was partly to prevent such abuses of kingly power, as I have suggested, that the Enlightenment emerged out of European history. It was partly in protest against such crimes that the whole glorious saga of the United States of America was acted out. Her Majesty's conduct then stands condemned in the public conscience!

ROOSEVELT: *(He is annoyed.)* Of course it does, Paine. But what are you getting at?

PAINE: *(He speaks quietly.)* Just this, Mr. President. That Father Aquinas here is guilty of the same crime of intention!

STEVE: What?

PAINE: Yes! He, too, justified *burning* heretics alive at the stake, beheading them, strangling them!

ROOSEVELT: *(He is troubled. He looks from Paine to Aquinas, then speaks.)* Is this true, Father?

AQUINAS: Yes. That was my view at the time. Today I might view the matter differently. Rightly or wrongly, there were reasons, you see, for the resort to capital punishment centuries ago.

There were few prisons, there was nothing like the legal machinery available today. Most of those accused, I suppose, were assumed to be guilty until proven innocent; and death was a common daily occurrence, from war, from sickness, from pestilence.

You see, everyone in the thirteenth century assumed it was permissible to execute those who harmed the body. Probably a majority are still of that opinion. But the heretic was, by definition, one who harmed the soul, by preaching false doctrines. So it seemed reasonable to consign him, too, to the execution chamber.

The man of each age can scarcely be more civilized than his culture permits. For whatever the point is worth, I observe that many of the leaders in the campaign to abolish capital punishment today are themselves clergymen.

ROOSEVELT: I see.

PAINE: And of course, Father, no doubt it was possible for you so easily to contemplate perhaps thirty or forty minutes of hideous suffering, in countless thousands of cases, because you already believed that millions of people are condemned by their all-loving God to spend untold millions and millions of years, indeed all eternity, in the literal flames of the mighty blast furnaces of Hell. I repeat, flames as real as this table. *(He raps on table.)* Do you deny it?

AQUINAS: Of course not, Mr. Paine. The Scriptures themselves tell us there is a hell, and we also have the word of Jesus Christ that it is so. Since you seem to be so familiar with my *Summa Theologica* you are no doubt aware that I have written that in order for the happiness of the saints in heaven to be more delightful to them—and that they may render more copious thanks to God for it—they are allowed to *see*, perfectly clearly, the sufferings of the damned.

ROOSEVELT: What, Father? Do you believe that those who go to heaven will literally be able to see some of their former friends, neighbors, perhaps loved ones, burning in fiery torment?

AQUINAS: Absolutely. The blessed in glory will have no pity for the damned.

ROOSEVELT: *(He frowns and shakes his head, clearly troubled by this pronouncement.)*

AQUINAS: But in pointing to what you, in your humanist conceit, regard as my errors, Mr. Paine, I must observe that you have done nothing to cast doubt on the truth of Christian doctrine itself.

PAINE: My argument is not with Christ, Father. It is with Aquinas. Speak for yourself.

AQUINAS: I shall. But it is impossible to separate my philosophy from the truth that Christ came to teach us; for my whole work, my whole life, was devoted to explaining to men the teachings of Jesus.

PAINE: Most of the teachings of Jesus, my friend, were wonderfully simple. Even children understand them. The same cannot be said of your works. Even the Franciscan theologian Duns Scotus said he could not understand some of your arguments!

AQUINAS: That does not prove they were false.

PAINE: You are right. It does not.

Father, it is said of you that you preferred not to think of yourself as a philosopher but rather as a theologian, is that correct?

AQUINAS: It is.

PAINE: I confess that I do not like such words: theologian, theology. Its meaning is—

AQUINAS: The science, doctrine, or knowledge of God.

PAINE: Precisely. And I say, therefore, that it is the most presumptuous word in the human language! Yes, presumptuous. How dare man—*little* man, *ignorant* man—presume to speak of his theories about God as certain knowledge! They are only theories, sir.

AQUINAS: Indeed, some speculation about God is theoretical, Mr. Paine, but theories, I repeat, are not necessarily false. And it is possible to speak of truthful science, doctrine, or knowledge of God.

PAINE: Such as.

AQUINAS: That God *exists*.

ROOSEVELT: Bully for you, father!

PAINE: I . . . well, all right, Aquinas. You've got me there. I, too, believe that this visible world was made by a Supreme Power, and I, too, call that power God. There may even be a few other statements about God that I would agree with.

CLEOPATRA: Oh, I see, gentlemen. Truth is simply what you two agree on, is that it?

PAINE: My point, Your Majesty, is that though there may be a few statements that can truthfully be made about God, those statements are damned few in number! But Aquinas here has written books by the dozens, and called it all *Theology*. *That*, I say, is the height of presumption!

AQUINAS: You have certain gifts for presumption yourself, Mr. Paine.

STEVE: Well, gentlemen, Your Majesty, if you will forgive me, perhaps we should change the subject. Very little is ever settled by heated argument about religion.

ROOSEVELT: Quite right.

STEVE: We have just a few minutes left. Tell me, Mr. Paine, what do you feel is the most significant thought about the American Revolution that you could suggest today.

PAINE: *(He thinks.)* The fact that it has not been *completed*. Of course no revolution has even been totally successful.

AQUINAS: Quite right. You see, revolution is a form of warfare; and since war is inevitably corrupting, it is one of the great tragedies of human experience that dangerous forces—as well as good, productive forces—are set loose by revolution.

PAINE: Yes. The French Revolution eventually succumbed to the worst sort of folly and terror. But even after the stormiest waters subside, revolutions always seem to lose much of the ground that they had earlier gained.

You know, it's funny, when I walked this earth I tended to think that if only we could be rid of George III, William Pitt, Robespierre, and others I regarded as evil, that perhaps the rest of men could more happily work out their destinies. But now I realize that the essential battleground is within the heart of every man. Each of us must resist apathy. Each of us must be on guard against our own prejudices. Each of us must refuse to be guided solely by our narrow, selfish interests.

AQUINAS: Yes, Mr. Paine, the worst dangers come not from men who are overwhelmingly evil. The worst work in the world is done by men who are good, most of the time, but who turn away from the light and choose the darkness when they see some immediate material advantage in doing so.

ROOSEVELT: Well spoken, Father.

STEVE: *(He strolls away from the table where the four guests continue to speak in subdued tones.)* I thank our distinguished guests. And I'm sure you join me in hoping they will visit us again.

On future programs of this series, I'm glad to report, you will be meeting such important personages from history as Charles Darwin, Emily Dickinson, Galileo, Ulysses S. Grant, Karl Marx, Sir Thomas More, Queen Marie Antoinette, and Attila the Hun.

All of us connected with "Meeting of Minds," by the way, are gratified by one particular sort of compliment the project has received. Naturally people who have an interest in history or philosophy would be pleased by our experiment. But we've been hearing from people who have said, in effect, "I've never had the slightest interest in history until seeing important leaders and heroes come to life on your program." That, of course, is the whole point. We wouldn't presume to instruct historians, philosophers, or other scholars. But if the rest of us can feel some sense of excitement, some sense of involvement with the ideas our guests express, some interest in the adventures they relate, then all of us connected with "Meeting of Minds" will be very happy.

SHOW #3

President Ulysses S. Grant

(JOSEPH EARLEY)

Queen Marie Antoinette

(JAYNE MEADOWS)

Sir Thomas More

(BERNARD BEHRENS)

Dr. Karl Marx

(LEON ASKIN)

&

Steve Allen

STEVE: Hello. Welcome again to "Meeting of Minds." Our first guest is a gentlemen whose picture you see every so often, if you're lucky enough to handle any fifty-dollar bills.

At the age of thirty-two he was decidedly a failure. He had resigned from the United States Army after being reprimanded, then failed at farming, selling real estate, and clerking in a customshouse. How did he move from these difficulties to become President of the United States? I'm sure he'll be glad to tell us this evening.

Ladies and gentlemen, President Ulysses S. Grant. *(Grant enters.) (Superimpose: Ulysses S. Grant, 1822–1885.)*

STEVE: Good evening, Mr. President.

GRANT: How do you do, sir.

STEVE: I see you chose to dress as General Grant rather than in civilian attire.

GRANT: Yes. I always saw myself as a military man rather than a politician.

STEVE: I see. Well, now, Mr. President, we've already mentioned your repeated failure in civilian life. And I understand you plan to tell us of your difficulties in a military career. As you know, you made many enemies during and after the Civil War. How in the world then were you ever elected president?

GRANT: *(He chuckles.)* Well, there were two main reasons, it seems to me. You see, the process by which we Americans elect presidents really has nothing to do with finding the best man in the country. If it were true that the most noble man, the best-educated man, the most dedicated and intelligent man were always elected president . . . well, I'm afraid very few of the men who have been our presidents would have qualified.

So the main reason I won is that the North had won the Civil War and I represented the Union cause. The people really weren't voting for me. They didn't know me that well. They were, in a sense, voting for themselves.

STEVE: I see.

Our next guest is one of the most fascinating women in history. Her enemies described her as frivolous, vain, even a traitor to her country. Her admirers have seen her as charming, courageous, and misunderstood. She was beheaded in the French Revolution, as was her husband, King Louis XVI. No doubt she'll be able to tell us a great deal about that revolution, and its causes.

Ladies and gentlemen, Her Majesty Queen Marie Antoinette of France. *(Marie enters.) (Superimpose: Marie Antoinette,
1755–1793.)*

STEVE: Your Majesty, we are honored to welcome you.

MARIE: It's my pleasure.

STEVE: Pardon me, Your Majesty. Are those little American flags I
see pinned in your hair?

MARIE: Thank you. I'm so glad you noticed.

STEVE: Who could help noticing such an impressive hairdo?

MARIE: You're very kind, but this is nothing compared to some of
the styles I used to wear.

STEVE: Really?

MARIE: Yes. This is only twelve inches high. There were times
when my wigs were eighteen inches high and on special occasions as high as three feet!

STEVE: My goodness. What kept them aloft?

MARIE: Oh, prayer. And lots of backcombings, artificial hair-
pieces, very long hairpins, or stiff pomade.

STEVE: You mean you had professional hairdressers, just as we
have today?

MARIE: Oh, it was at Versailles, Mr. Allen, that some of your
modern hairdos were invented. The pompadour style, for instance, came from Madame de Pompadour. You see, we celebrated the events of the day by our hairstyles. I once had a
whole ocean-in-a-storm up there. And when your American
Revolution was the topic of conversation in Paris, Mr. President, we celebrated it with our hairdos.

GRANT: How did you ever climb into your carriages, Your
Majesty, with such high hairdresses?

MARIE: We just pulled up our skirts and knelt down, Mr. President.
Even the ceilings in the boxes in the theatres had to be recon-
structed into arches to accommodate us.

STEVE: Of course the young girls today don't have the time to fix
their hair as elaborately as you did, Your Majesty.

MARIE: No, poor things.

GRANT: They would do well, however, to study the femininity and
charm of the eighteenth century.

STEVE: Of the upper classes, at least. It must have been more
difficult for the poor.

MARIE: Of course, at Versailles we had nothing to do all day long,
the men included, but beautify ourselves.

STEVE: You were sort of the original jet set, weren't you?

MARIE: The what?

STEVE: Never mind. Your Majesty, what was the court life really like?

MARIE: At Versailles, you mean? Ours was the most sumptuous palace in the whole world. We had over a hundred rooms and two thousand beautiful horses in the stables and—

STEVE: Two thousand horses?

MARIE: Yes, and about four thousand servants, all dressed in gorgeous livery.

STEVE: I imagine life must have been very formal at Versailles.

MARIE: Oh, very. The ladies and gentlemen of the court were always dressed in the most gorgeous brocades, silks, and, of course, exquisite jewels; and well, we just danced or gambled—I loved to gamble—or masqueraded all night long in those ballrooms with their beautiful crystal chandeliers, and everywhere gleaming silver and gold. It was very extravagant. Yes, Versailles was the most extravagant and the most elegant and the most utterly boring place in the world.

STEVE: *(He and Grant laugh.)* Versailles boring?

MARIE: Oh, utterly. In fact, it bored me so much I persuaded my husband, the King, to give me my own little palace, the Petite Trianon, not far from Versailles, where I spent much of my time entertaining my most intimate friends.

STEVE: Excuse me, Your Majesty. Before we go any further I want to introduce our other guests who I know will also want to hear your stories of Versailles.

MARIE: Well, one of them at least I shall be most pleased to meet.

STEVE: Ah. And that would of course be the distinguished Lord Chancellor under King Henry VIII, perhaps the most honest man in England in his day. His courage and strength have been an inspiration to many down through the ages. Sir Thomas More! *(More enters.) (Superimpose: Sir Thomas More, 1478–1535.)*

STEVE: Welcome, your Lordship.

MORE: Thank you, sir. How kind of you to invite me.

STEVE: You know, it's just occurred to me: Her Majesty was beheaded, by the people of Paris. We might say by the left wing. You were beheaded, at the order of King Henry VIII, by, we might say, the right wing. So there can be danger from either democracy or monarchy.

MORE: Oh, indeed, sir. We live on a singularly dangerous planet.

But we are well advised to give more thought to how we live than to how we may die.

STEVE: Which brings to mind our next guest. Although he had the interests of the poor and oppressed at heart when developing his philosophy, his followers have nevertheless been responsible for executing millions in some of the nations which have come under their control. I'm sure he will want to comment on that painful fact.

　　To describe him as controversial would be to put it mildly. He is revered by millions and, with equal fervor, hated by millions of others. He and his associate, Friedrich Engels, published a pamphlet in 1848, and our world has not been the same since. Eighteen forty-eight was itself a year when Europe trembled with revolutionary ferment. It was the year when *The Communist Manifesto* was written by our next guest.

　　Ladies and gentlemen, the founder of the most influential mass movement since Christianity, Dr. Karl Marx. *(Marx enters.) (Superimpose: Karl Marx, 1818–1883.)*

MARX: *(As he seats himself, he is startled that a few in the audience are booing.)*

STEVE: I'm afraid, Dr. Marx, that such a response from our audience is inevitable, given the political history of the last half century. In any event I assure you, you will be permitted to speak at length and freely here this evening.

MARX: *(Somewhat sarcastically.)* Thank you, sir. You referred, in your introduction, to the fact that I am hated, by some. Presumably they hate me out of concern for their own freedoms. But . . . there is one point I should like my opponents to understand.

　　Your Majesty, did the common man—in France in your day—have the freedom to say who would rule him? Did he control very much at all of his own destiny?

MARIE: *(She is flustered.)* Oh. Why . . . I . . . I'm sure I don't know. The people loved us . . . but I . . . I never concerned myself with such questions.

MARX: *(He turns, in disgust, to "the jury.")* You see what the problem was.

　　But I wrote my document in a time when the modern freedoms you Americans love to boast of were largely unknown. Prussia then had no freedom of speech, no freedom of assembly, no freedom of the press, no trial by jury, and no Parliament. It was dangerous to oppose the Prussian state, and the common people were poor and oppressed.

Perhaps now you can understand that what Voltaire once said of God might also have been said of me.

STEVE: What was that, sir?

MARX: That if I had not existed, it would have been necessary to invent me!

STEVE: Well, now, the French Revolution helped pave the way to the workers' uprisings of your century, Dr. Marx, so let's put a few questions to Her Majesty.

If you will forgive us, Your Majesty, many today know what was merely the last chapter of your personal drama, the tragedy of your public execution in Paris in 1793. But, of course, to understand the conclusion of your story we would have to know of the introductory chapters of your life, would we not?

MARIE: Oh, yes. I see.

Well, anyway, I was of the Austrian House of the Hapsburgs. And while we're clearing up misconceptions, gentlemen—if I may satisfy the morbid curiosity about such matters—I did not say "Let them eat cake"; and as for the infamous "diamond necklace"—which I expect someone will bring up—I not only never owned it, I never saw it. And I was not a nymphomaniac!

STEVE: But you mentioned gambling, Your Majesty. Isn't it true that you lost millions at the gaming tables?

MARIE: (She smiles coquettishly.) Well, yes. Now that is true. Do you know I once gambled the whole day and night of All Saints' Day.

MORE: (In mock horror.) All Saints' Day, Your Majesty?

MARIE: Yes, wasn't that dreadful?

MARX: Your Majesty, you were born in 1755, were you not?

MARIE: How flattering of you to know, Dr. Marx.

MARX: Yes, on a date which is perhaps better recalled as that of the great tragedy of Portugal, the Lisbon earthquake. It took place, gentlemen, on the morning of All Saints' Day just after High Mass had begun in all the churches of the city. Perhaps as many as thirty thousand innocent people were killed, most of them as they worshipped.

Your Majesty, do you believe that Nature is the hand of God?

MARIE: I? Well . . . yes.

MARX: Then perhaps you can explain to us why God was so cruel to the good Christians of Lisbon.

MARIE: *(She is shocked.)* I . . . God, cruel?

MORE: Natural disasters, Dr. Marx, are accidents, not necessarily examples of divine intervention, as you know perfectly well.

MARX: Of course. Perhaps you could enlighten the majority of your fellow Christians on the point. Your Bible clearly teaches that natural calamities are inflicted by the Deity. And you lawyers refer to such disasters as "acts of God," do you not?

MORE: Yes, but the term has only poetic meaning.

Your Majesty, your mother, the Empress Maria Theresa of Austria, was a remarkable figure, wasn't she?

MARIE: Oh, Sir Thomas, if I'd had her knowledge of political affairs, the history of my time might have been very different. But I was not the sort of person who creates important historic events. It was the other way around, I'm afraid. For example, it was the alliance between France and Austria that led to my marriage.

MARX: It led also to your importance in history.

MARIE: *(Not too brightly.)* Thank you, sir.

GRANT: Do you recall how the French and Austrian alliance came about, Your Majesty?

MARIE: I think it was created chiefly by my mother, Mr. President.

MARX: To understand this "diplomatic revolution," gentlemen, you must remind yourself of that remarkable historical drama, the Protestant Reformation.

GRANT: The Reformation? What's that got to do with the price of eggs?

MORE: Well, you see, Mr. Grant, it was the Reformation that ended the Renaissance—that flowering of culture, of art, of music, architecture, of sculpture, literature—that great outburst of Catholic creativity, which still stands as the highest of artistic achievements.

MARX: Well now, Sir Thomas, the Reformation was a reaction against corruption in the Church, was it not?

MORE: Obviously, Dr. Marx, but it left a Europe divided, suspicious, and hostile.

MARX: Oh, come, come. Europe was already divided. And are you suggesting, Sir Thomas, that there should never have been a Reformation?

MORE: No, Dr. Marx, reform was necessary. But it should have come from within the Church.

MARX: Oh, certainly it should have. But it did not. The Protestant

Reformation was the price the Roman Church paid for its own sins, until the Catholic Counter-Reformation.

MORE: It might be so construed, but at the end Europe was divided—the Protestant powers against the Catholic.

MARIE: Yes, and that dreadful man Frederick the Great came upon the scene as an opponent of the Catholic nations.

GRANT: Your Majesty, as a general, I've always considered Frederick one of the great military leaders of history.

MARX: It's interesting that you so admired Frederick, Mr. Grant. I understand that your nation has fought two great wars against the forces of Germany, which is to say, forces largely unleashed by Frederick the Prussian.

Before his day there was such a thing as honor in war, and in negotiation. Frederick was contemptuous of the traditional morality of war.

MARIE: Yes. My mother, Empress Marie Theresa, felt that war is such a horrible institution that some things must absolutely be done to civilize it.

MORE: Quite so, Your Majesty. The rules of the civilized conduct of war should be somewhat like those established for dealing with criminal offenses by individuals. You do not rush up to a man on the street when you think he has committed a crime and strike him dead on the spot. You arrest him, you send him to trial, give him the opportunity to speak in his own defense. Only then, if he is convicted, is a sentence passed. Just so, in war, there should be some semblance of reason and civilization. All is not fair, in either love or war.

STEVE: Speaking of war, let's put some questions to the military man here this evening, General Grant.

MARX: Yes. How did life prepare you for battle, General?

GRANT: (He flourishes a cigar.) Well, I was born in a small cabin in Point Pleasant, Ohio. My father, Jesse Root Grant, was descended from the Puritans of the Massachusetts Colony.

STEVE: The Puritans?

GRANT: That's right. His business was tanning leather. One wise thing he did was see to it that I got a fair education.

MORE: Where were you educated?

GRANT: Well, in 1839, when I was seventeen, my father arranged an appointment for me to the United States Military Academy at West Point.

STEVE: You must have been very pleased and proud.

GRANT: Not at all! I hated the whole idea of going to West Point. I went only because of the train ride. I knew it would take me to Philadelphia and New York, at that time the two largest cities in the country. After having enjoyed myself for several days in each city, I took the train to West Point. I remember hoping that the train would have an accident so I wouldn't have to go, but the next four years were spent at West Point.

MORE: Where, I assume, you distinguished yourself?

GRANT: The hell you say; I barely made the grade. Since I'd done plenty of hard farm labor I was handy around horses, so I did well as a cavalryman. But I graduated in 1843, only twenty-first in a class of thirty-nine, and—wouldn't you know it?—the army sent me into the infantry instead of the cavalry.

STEVE: Some things never change. What happened then?

GRANT: Oh, I knocked around the country a couple of years, in Missouri and Louisiana; but nothing very interesting happened to me till 1845 when I accompanied Zachary Taylor to Texas, and later went on to serve in the invasion of Mexico.

STEVE: I understand, Mr. President, you felt that it was an immoral war.

GRANT: Yes, we had no right going in there. We'd already taken Texas away from the Mexicans. Now President Polk wanted New Mexico and California. If I had the moral courage I had later, I would have resigned.

STEVE: By the way, I happen to know, Sir Thomas, what the President might be too modest to mention: that during those days he served with great bravery and was twice cited for gallantry under fire.

GRANT: Well, that's what a good soldier is supposed to do, isn't it?

Anyway, things were going pretty well for me until 1852. At that point I'd been married for four years to Julia Dent and we were stationed at Sackets Harbor, New York. But my regiment was transferred to the Pacific Coast, and my dear wife wasn't able to accompany me because of the hardships of traveling across country in those days.

MARIE: What a pity.

GRANT: Thank you, Your Majesty. Well, I got to drinking a little more than I should have and was a little hotheaded, I suppose, in dealing with some of my superior officers.

Anyway, in July 1854 I gave up on military life and went back to my wife and children, as a civilian. That brings us to the years of failure you mentioned, Mr. Allen. I couldn't make it in the real estate business, I failed as a farmer.

In fact, if it hadn't been for my two brothers offering me a job as a simple clerk in their leather goods store in Galena, Illinois, I probably would have gone to the poorhouse.

STEVE: Incredible.

MORE: But what was it, Mr. President, that changed the course of your fortune?

GRANT: It was war, Sir Thomas, which, as we know, is an ill-wind that always blows a little good for a few, although it means tragedy to millions.

The Civil War finally broke out in the United States. That meant that military men were in short supply and high demand. I saw a chance to get back into action, doing something that at least I knew how to do. I thought perhaps I might take command of a regiment. I began to drill a volunteer company right there in Galena, Illinois.

MORE: And thereafter things went well for you?

GRANT: Not by a long shot. My so-called volunteers were a mutinous, unruly bunch. Most men, you see, aren't any natural great shakes as fighters. The only way you can turn men into good soldiers is either to make them professionals at the trade, or to get 'em angry.

STEVE: How did you solve that problem?

GRANT: I didn't. Fortunately, just at that point, I was promoted to the rank of Brigadier General and put into a regular command at Cairo, Illinois, on the Ohio River.

MORE: I wonder what it is, Mr. Grant, that earns for one commander a superior reputation, when another officer, of let us say generally equal competence, is denied such honors.

GRANT: (Thoughtfully.) Oh, God, I don't know, if you'll pardon my language. Success in many fields, I suspect, is a matter of getting the breaks. My big break was the Civil War.

STEVE: But not all Civil War generals, in the North or the South, emerged from the contest with such high honors.

GRANT: Yeah, that's true. Maybe one thing I had going for me was that I didn't like to lose. You see, I'd lost so damned much already, and it seemed to me that war was my one last chance to prove that I wasn't a complete failure as a human being. So I was determined, right from the start, to fight like hell.

MARX: But when we say that a general fights like hell, or fights to any degree, Mr. President, isn't there some confusion in terms? Isn't it really the individual soldiers under his command who do the fighting, and dying?

GRANT: Oh, absolutely. But a general sets an example for his men. If he's a scrapper, they generally are, too.

STEVE: But Mr. President, if I may say so, you don't strike any of us here as a particularly pugnacious person.

GRANT: Well, I wouldn't be proud if I was. A hotheaded officer can get his men into trouble! Personally, I hated war!

STEVE: You did?

GRANT: Yes. I couldn't even stand the sight of blood, from the early days working in my father's leather-tanning factory. Hell, I couldn't even eat steak unless it was well done.

MORE: Remarkable.

GRANT: I couldn't kill animals either. And you know, I never carried a sidearm during the war. I think there's something a little odd about men who relish using weapons.

MORE: I could not agree with you more.

GRANT: But you've got to understand that war itself is a kind of a madness. War means killing. A soldier is a man who is hired to kill. Bill Sherman was right when he said war is hell. It's a miserable, stinking business.

MARX: A strangely modern view of war, wouldn't you say, More?

MORE: Yes, but through all time war must have seemed like hell to the poor foot soldier.

MARX: And yet, in all ages, some men have chosen to take up the bloody business as a profession. Why?

MORE: Apparently some men have natural gifts for fighting and killing, just as others are inclined to science or the arts or to government.

STEVE: Your Majesty, we were discussing the background of events in Europe leading to the alliance between Austria and France. At what point in that story then do we come to your personal drama?

MARIE: (Girlishly.) Well, Mr. Allen, I guess that would be at the time of my birth, 1755. Louis XV ruled France, and he was at war with the English, you know. My mother, who hoped for an alliance with France, was aided by Madame Pompadour. She was the mistress of Louis XV.

MORE: Were you close to your mother at the time?

MARIE: No. My father was dead and the war occupied all my

mother's time and attention. Mama saw me and my sister Caroline formally only about once a week.

GRANT: Who took care of you?

MARIE: We were reared by a good-natured German governess, the Countess of Brandweiss.

MORE: Were you well educated, Your Majesty?

MARIE: (Embarrassed laugh.) Oh, no, Sir Thomas; hardly at all. Oh, from my music teacher, Gluck, I learned a little something. I hated reading, though. It bored me. No, I ran rather wild, I'm afraid. I had no serious interests, no real training for anything.

STEVE: Was yours a dull childhood, Your Majesty?

MARIE: Oh, never dull. Oh, no! Life in our old palace in Vienna was wonderful, with my brothers, my sister. I remember one night when Mozart—he was only a little child of six himself at the time—came to play a concert for us. On his way to the piano he slipped on the highly polished floor. He didn't hurt himself. (She laughs, remembering.) I lifted him up, and then sat enthralled as he played his beautiful music for us. What a genius!

MORE: Six years old!

MARIE: Yes.

GRANT: Your Majesty, was there much difference in that day between the Austrian and the French courts?

MARIE: Less than you might think, Mr. President. The French culture was dominant all over the continent, and I think the court in Vienna was really more French than German. As a young girl I was myself very taken with French manners and styles. My hair was brushed in the French manner, my gowns were French. Even my name was changed from the Austrian Maria Antonia to Marie Antoinette.

STEVE: Now just how did your fortunes become involved with those of the French court, Your Majesty?

MARIE: Well, in 1765 the Dauphin, the son of Louis XV, died. The heir to the throne then was the King's grandson, Louis, a child of eleven. At once a plan was set afoot by my mother, and her adviser Kaunitz, that this boy and I were to be married. Kaunitz was rather like your Kissinger of the modern day.

STEVE: Had Louis XV been a good king?

MARIE: Well, I always liked him.

MARX: He was not particularly gifted at affairs of state. Then, too, the Seven Years' War had weakened France greatly.

MORE: Do you think, Your Majesty, that Louis's selection of

Madame Du Barry as mistress was an important part of the long process of decay?

MARIE: You are quite right, Sir Thomas. His earlier mistress, Madame Pompadour, was charming. But after her death came Du Barry, who was a common slut!

GRANT: You don't say.

MARIE: Madame Pompadour had been popular in the court of Versailles. Du Barry's presence there was a scandal!

MARX: But, at least, by that year, 1770, the French-Austrian alliance had been consummated by your marriage.

GRANT: Was your marriage a happy one, Your Majesty?

MARIE: Happy? Mr. President, I was only fifteen years old. I had not wanted to leave my home in Vienna. Ours was a marriage in name only. My husband, you see, was impotent. Eventually his impediment was corrected by an operation. But for seven long years I lived through a nightmare.

STEVE: But, if you don't mind my asking, Your Majesty, did you love Louis?

MARIE: (Evasively.) I was not born to love. I was born to be a queen.

MORE: But, Your Majesty, there was one who, in time, you came to love, was there not?

MARIE: Yes, Sir Thomas. He was Count Axel de Fersen, a visitor to Versailles from Sweden. We were both just eighteen when we met, at a masked ball. He didn't know who I was, at first. I thought he was the handsomest man I had ever seen.

STEVE: You loved parties and masked balls, didn't you, Your Majesty?

MARIE: Oh, yes. Behind a mask, my identity unknown, I felt a delicious sense of . . . of freedom, which my position otherwise denied me.

STEVE: How do you explain, Your Majesty, that the world knew nothing of your relationship with Fersen, the love of your life, until about one hundred years later when your love letters to him were found in Sweden?

MARIE: Out of respect for both His Majesty and Count de Fersen, sir, I was as discreet as possible. Only a few intimates were aware of the situation.

MARX: I forget what year it was that the old King Louis died.

MARIE: Seventeen seventy-four, sir, the year I became Queen of France.

MARX: Ah, yes. The day of his death is remembered better here on the American continent as that of the Boston Tea Party.

GRANT: Is that right? Your Majesty, did the people miss the King, despite his faults?

MARIE: Oh, yes, Mr. President. The people had great affection for the monarchy. It was almost as if they owned us, rather than the other way around. They had much more ready access to us than you have today to your presidents and prime ministers.

STEVE: Is that right?

MARIE: Yes. We lived a highly visible life. We took our meals in an enormous open hall, sometimes watched by thousands of the populace. When we prayed and worshipped, it was done in public.

Even what you would today consider our most intimate acts were, some of them, performed before an audience, as it were.

STEVE: What do you mean?

MARIE: We were dressed and undressed, not in complete privacy, but in the presence of a retinue of servants and hangers-on. Even the births of royal children, all my children, were witnessed by great numbers of people, who would crowd into my bedchamber to watch the event.

GRANT: Fascinating.

MARIE: As a Queen I literally could not take a sip of water, even in the middle of the night, by myself. Custom dictated that I accept the cup from the hand of the highest-ranking woman in the room.

MARX: Did it ever enter your mind, Your Majesty, that such empty rituals and customs would in time destroy the people's respect for the monarchy?

MARIE: Nonsense, Dr. Marx, the people adored the rituals and customs!

MORE: Yes, Dr. Marx. Consider the ceremonies we perform when a loved one has died. The rituals are more for the living than the dead. If we took them away, it would be difficult for many to properly act out their sorrow.

In the case of the monarchy, rituals and manners aided the people to express their respect for royalty. I understand that in today's Marxist nations there is still room for pomp and ceremony.

STEVE: Well, now, may we discuss the subject of revolution? What about the philosophers whose ideas led to the French Revolution?

MARX: There's no question but that the views of the French Enlightenment thinkers helped bring about the Revolution. But we must not overlook economic factors. You see, when Her Majesty and King Louis XVI ruled at Versailles, the financial system of the French nation was in a terrible state.

MARIE: I'm afraid, sir, that I knew little or nothing of this at the time.

MARX: So one would assume.

MARIE: You must realize, in 1776 I was only twenty-one and unfortunately little interested in even such important events as the American Revolution, Mr. President.

GRANT: Mmm.

MORE: Your Majesty, to digress for a moment, do you think your Austrian birth had something to do with the idea, then common in France, that you were not entirely loyal to French interests?

MARIE: Perhaps.

MARX: Your question, sir, relates to the problem of Bavaria. In 1778, Your Majesty, your home court of Vienna—then ruled by your brother Joseph—laid claim to Bavaria. But the Prussians in Berlin also wanted it.

MARIE: Yes, my mother, the Empress, wanted me to help bring in France on the side of Austria. I pleaded with Louis and he agreed to help the Austrian cause. This, of course, required a great expenditure of money, so I was later accused of "paying out French gold" for matters that were of no direct concern to France.

But much of that was forgotten when, shortly thereafter, the court learned I was to give birth to an heir.

GRANT: Good for you!

MARIE: (She smiles.) On the nineteenth of December the court was invited to witness the birth, and many hundreds came from miles around. The child, unfortunately for our hopes, was a girl. The people were disappointed with me.

MORE: You did subsequently bear a son.

MARIE: Yes, two. I remember, in 1780, when my second child was born, I said to my attendants: "I've been a good patient . . . tell me the truth."

I feared, you see, that another daughter had been born. At that moment the King walked in and said to me very sweetly, "The Dauphin begs leave to come in." Ooh . . . it was one of the happiest moments of my life.

MARX: Your Majesty, wasn't the dramatic incident of a certain diamond necklace greatly responsible for your unpopularity in Paris?

MARIE: I might have known, Dr. Marx, that you would bring that up! Though you, as a historian, must know I was unjustly accused. I won't bore you with the sordid details—

MORE: Please do.

MARIE: (She smiles.) Well, a terrible woman named La Motte took advantage of her lover, that incredible ignoramus the Cardinal de Rohan; and, by forging certain letters, made believe that I wanted to purchase the enormously expensive necklace. It was all utterly untrue.

MORE: Your Majesty, that a cardinal should also be a fool and a cheat was, alas, not so unusual at that time, was it?

MARIE: Regretfully, no. Scandals in the Church were common; and the intellectuals who attacked the Faith were able to support their arguments by pointing to the many churchmen who, one must concede, were themselves sinful and power-hungry men.

GRANT: Your Majesty, what do you think were the reasons for the French Revolution?

MARIE: Oh, dear me! I'm not at all sure. I would imagine there were a great many causes for such a disaster. But I really think the hostility of some members of the French nobility had a great deal to do with it.

STEVE: For example?

MARIE: (She tries to think.) Well, let me see—

MARX: The Baron de Montesquieu, for one. His book, *Spirit of the Laws*, which he had published in 1748 had bitterly attacked the French monarchy.

MARIE: Yes, then there was that dreadful François Marie Arouet, who wrote under the name of Voltaire. He spent much of his time in England and Geneva, since he dared not live in France after what he had written about the monarchy, and about the Church.

MARX: Yes. Voltaire favored both democracy and religious freedom. And, of course, the French Catholic monarchy could not abide such ideas.

MORE: Perhaps later, Herr Marx, you will comment on the status of democracy and religious freedom in the present-day Communist nations.

MARX: (He is furious.) Most assuredly!

MARIE: Another terrible troublemaker was Jean Jacques Rousseau. He was a disturbed and confused man.

MARX: Rousseau had the idea that while the old institutions were not to be trusted, neither was the philosophical emphasis on the power of reason.

MARIE: Yes, he wrote a silly book called *The Social Contract*. I wouldn't read it, of course. Well, to be honest, I never finished any book. But my friends told me that this ignoramus—in a day when there was hardly enough civilization to go around—actually had the gall to attack civilization, claiming it corrupted the "natural goodness" of man's nature. Oh, if ever there has been a more nonsensical idea, I have yet to hear of it.

GRANT: *(He chuckles.)* Just what was it about Rousseau that so annoyed you, Your Majesty?

MARIE: Why, his lack of respect for the nobility, for the monarchy, for all the important institutions.

MARX: You see, Mr. President, Rousseau paraded the word liberty before the people, as if it were a magic emblem equal in power to the crucifix itself. Indeed, who could claim that liberty is evil? But the word has no meaning unless we ask the question, Liberty to do what? Rousseau flattered the common man by telling him that he was some sort of potential ideal free spirit.

MARIE: We can observe that quite the reverse is true by looking directly at some of the common men we have the misfortune to encounter.

While I am very far from being a philosopher, gentlemen, I do understand, I think, what virtue is. And what it is not. And I know that Monsieur Rousseau was a thief and a scoundrel!

MORE: Would you give us any specifics, Your Majesty?

MARIE: If you insist. Rousseau took up with a poor woman named Therese Le Vasseur, a maidservant. He lived with her for the rest of his life, and she bore him five children, each of which he took at birth to a foundling hospital!

Rousseau professed to admire "the noble savage." He himself was savage without being in the least noble.

MORE: Are you going to sit idly by, Dr. Marx, without defending one of your heroes?

MARX: *(He smiles.)* It is quite true that I based my philosophy on that certain moral superiority which, I assumed, resides in the masses and not in the depraved and debauched aristocracy. No reflection on present company.

MARIE: Oh, I was called far worse in my day, Dr. Marx.

MORE: As you look at today's unrest and bloodshed, Dr. Marx, does your faith, your romantic opinion of the masses, ever waver at all?

MARX: *(He sighs sadly.)* I confess that at times it does. But see here, More, you cannot blame me for all the crimes and follies committed in my name during the past hundred years. Unless, that is, you would also blame Christ for the massacres of the Crusades, the slaughter of the Huguenots, the terror of the Spanish Inquisition, or the burning of witches!

MORE: The atrocities committed by Christians, sir, are perpetrated by those who forget or distort the teaching of Christ. Were the crimes and atrocities of Stalin perpetrated in accordance with your principles, Herr Marx, or in opposition to them?

MARX: The blood of the millions of Ukrainian peasants and others killed by Stalin is on his head, not mine! I preached a doctrine designed to bring men together, not set them apart.

I thought that if men could be emancipated from the pressure of superstition and tyranny, the human mind would exercise its capacity for rational thought, and the enjoyment of beauty, and the good simple things of life.

I argued that the system of private property, and the selfish exploitation that grew out of it, was what made some men poor and miserable, and others rich and selfish. Abolish private ownership of important property, let the common people, the working class, assume control of a country, and all classes will disappear. Men will be equal in brotherhood.

Oh, and may I respectfully point out, Sir Thomas, that despite your apparently quite successful appeal to the emotions of the ladies and gentlemen present, there is a logical inconsistency in your argument.

MORE: What is that, Dr. Marx?

MARX: You have quite correctly stated that you personally are willing to concede that the atrocities committed by the followers of Christ were *not* committed in accordance with His teachings. Then you asked when *my* followers will be prepared to make the same concession.

But the inconsistency, my friend, is this: it is utterly irrelevant that you *personally* are willing, as a Christian, to make your gracious concession, because you personally were *not*

THEODORE ROOSEVELT

All photographs by Robbie Robertson

CLEOPATRA

FATHER THOMAS AQUINAS

THOMAS PAINE

ULYSSES S. GRANT

MARIE ANTOINETTE AND SIR THOMAS MORE

KARL MARX

CHARLES   DARWIN   AND   GALILEO   GALILEI

ATTILA   THE   HUN   AND   EMILY   DICKINSON

guilty of the atrocities. For the concession to be *convincing* it would have to come from those who *perpetrated* the many crimes by Christian forces.

GRANT: Well, now wait a minute, Marx. It seems to me that the fact that Sir Thomas is himself a good Christian is quite sufficient to permit him to make the statement that—

MORE: Thank you, Mr. President, but Dr. Marx is quite right. It would indeed have been better that those *guilty* of the crimes of Christendom confessed the error of their ways. But the historical record is clear that they never did. The crimes were, God help us, *defended.*

Would you nevertheless join me, Dr. Marx, in agreeing on the ancient truism that two wrongs do not make a right?

MARX: I would.

MORE: Then I am content. For what I am concerned to do here is insist on the moral verities. But I believe, Your Majesty, that it becomes easier to at least understand Marx's philosophy if we consider it not as something foreign to Western tradition, but regard it rather as a Christian heresy.

After all, the Scriptures do tell us that love of money is the root of evil. We Christians, therefore, ought not to worship money and its power as much as some of us do. It is clear that Karl Marx would have lived and died in obscurity had not the Christians of nineteenth-century Europe, and those before them, failed to live up to their moral responsibilities.

MARIE: What do you mean?

MORE: Had there not been so much suffering, so much poverty, so much degradation, so much social injustice in Christian Europe, Karl Marx would never have been moved to issue his mighty roar of social protest.

STEVE: Your Majesty, is there any way of knowing when the French Revolution actually began?

MARIE: Probably not. Although, as I look back now, it seems to me that one of the first trumpet blasts of the Revolution had been sounded in 1784 when the Count de Beaumarchais presented his play *The Marriage of Figaro.* It was a satire of the established order and an enormous success. No doubt it does not seem startling today to stage a drama about a servant outwitting his master, but it was a daring theatrical stroke at the time.

MARX: Then why did you produce and act in the first public

performance of it in your own theatre at the Trianon?

MARIE: I know it was foolish of me, Dr. Marx, but it was such a lovely part.

STEVE: At what point, Your Majesty, would you say the battle to preserve the monarchy was finally lost?

MARIE: *(She thinks.)* I believe that would be in 1787, sir. There was widespread depression. Even God and Nature seemed to conspire against us. Oh, no, pardon me. It was 1788. The harvests were poor, and I was told there was severe hunger in many parts of the country. I remember now . . . we celebrated it by putting little cakes and cookies in our hairdos.

GRANT: Good God!

STEVE: Are you serious? You celebrated the hunger of the poor people of France?

MARX: Yes, gentlemen, it did happen. And, does not the story tell its own moral? Revolution in France had to come, just as it did in your own country.

And may I remind you, Your Majesty, that your government was bankrupt. The situation had deteriorated so badly that the King was advised to call a meeting of the Estates-General, the French Parliament, which had not met since 1614.

The Parliament became unruly and the walls began to crumble. The Revolution was under way.

GRANT: Was it the lower classes, Your Majesty, that were chiefly responsible for rising against you?

MARIE: No, Mr. Grant. The people loved us. Initially it was jealous members of the nobility who were the troublemakers!

MARX: Yes, Mr. President, and to a considerable extent it was the bourgeoisie, the middle classes of the larger cities, who gradually emerged as a strong force contrary to the crown. These people were becoming educated, powerful, and ambitious. Naturally they resented the empty-headed parasites at Versailles.

I do not refer to present company, Your Majesty.

MARIE: Oh, I don't care! I was hated for my Austrian birth and—

MARX: If you'll forgive me, Your Majesty, I believe there was one other factor that assumed considerable importance.

MARIE: Oh? And what was that?

MARX: Your frequent and questionable interference in matters of state.

MARIE: *(Angrily.)* Dr. Marx, may I remind you that I was the Queen of France! And that my husband the King could boast no more than a mediocre intellect and could not make a decision! What wife would not offer her husband advice in such circumstances?

MORE: Just when was it, Your Majesty, that the first waves of the Revolution actually burst upon the Palace of Versailles?

MARIE: That, Sir Thomas, was in the autumn of 1789. It was the mobs of Paris which came to threaten and endanger us. It was terrifying! I had never before seen the people raised in anger against us.

I shall never forget the sounds of crowds roaring, near and far, shots being fired, the vision of smoke and flame in the distance. And then, at last, the heavy tramp of marching feet as a great army of mostly women, mind you, who had walked for over six hours from Paris, in the rain—

STEVE: Why women?

MARIE: I don't know. It was all very confusing.

GRANT: I've heard that those who fomented this revolutionary act had deliberately prevented the delivery of bread to Paris for two days, knowing that housewives would be furious.

MARX: Then, too, as Her Majesty had no way of knowing at the time, the leaders knew that the royal troops would never fire on unarmed women.

MARIE: Well, those housewives—or fishwives and prostitutes, as some of them were—were more vicious than the men in the vulgar, shocking things they shouted at us! I later learned that some in the crowd were men dressed as women, who came along as agitators.

STEVE: Who was behind all this?

MARX: Many men, Mr. Allen, including two quite well known to Her Majesty—the Duke of Orléans and the Count of Provence, a member of the King's own family.

MARIE: The true traitors!

GRANT: Pardon me, Your Majesty. I recall that the great military hero, Lafayette—who distinguished himself in our American Revolution—that he tried to help you. Just what did happen there?

MARIE: Lafayette didn't arrive until midnight, Mr. President. He had twenty thousand men, but the situation was already out of hand. Having stormed the great prison of Paris, the Bastille, the people were seized by a combination of jubilation and savagery.

His Majesty graciously received a small group of women representing the mob, and calmed them by his presence and fairness. But at five in the morning hundreds of drunken insurgents broke into the palace shouting "To the Queen's apartments!" They rushed to my quarters, murdered my bodyguards, and started to break down my doors.

STEVE: Good Lord.

MARIE: Fortunately I was awakened by a lady-in-waiting. I rushed immediately from bed, without having time to dress, to the King's apartments!

MORE: Was he awake?

MARIE: I don't know. We pounded on the doors till our knuckles were almost covered with blood, while behind us we could hear the vulgar shouts of the invaders and my furniture being smashed as the mob searched for me. At the last moment the doors were finally opened and our lives were saved!

GRANT: Had they come to kill the King?

MARX: No, not at all. They merely wanted to reassert that they owned the King, that he was their property, and that he should rule them from the intimacy of Paris rather than from the distant Palace at Versailles.

MARIE: *(Bitterly.)* Oh, really, Dr. Marx! I tell you, those savages would have torn me limb from limb.

STEVE: Well, what did happen?

MARIE: They demanded first that Louis appear on his balcony, and then that I appear. Lafayette explained to us that we could not avoid this painful act. We were simply terrified when we saw muskets in the crowd below, aimed at our heads. And then the most peculiar thing happened.

STEVE: What was that?

MARIE: Why, when this wild mob, which had just murdered my bodyguards and threatened my life, saw His Majesty, and then saw me, they actually cheered us. Long Live the King! Long Live the Queen! It was very strange.

MARX: Why, of course, at that point they merely wanted you to rule from the former palace, the Tuileries, in Paris.

STEVE: You later attempted escape, didn't you?

MARIE: Yes. Mirabeau had warned us, "The King does not run away from his people." But, what can I say, we were afraid for our lives.

We escaped in a magnificent new carriage which my dear Count de Fersen had had built for us. It was large enough for the five members of our family. All our meals on the way were served on the royal silver service.

STEVE: Do you think now that traveling in such luxury was perhaps a mistake?

MARIE: I suppose so, since we were recognized along the way. When we had almost reached the frontier, when we were almost safe, we were recognized and captured.

MARX: In April of 1792 the French Assembly voted for war against Austria. As an Austrian Her Majesty was now regarded as one of the enemy, and her cause became utterly hopeless.

MARIE: In my panic I prayed to God that vengeance would be taken for the provocations we had received from France! Never till that moment had I been more proud to have been born a German!

We were imprisoned in the tower of the Temple. From that moment on, our existence was a continual nightmare. In the streets the people were still bloodthirsty and half mad. One afternoon the mob dragged the body of one of my best friends they had murdered, Madame de Lamballe. The head had been chopped from the nude body. Someone stuck it up on a long pole and thrust it up toward our windows! The King tried to prevent my seeing it, but too late. At the sight I fainted.

MORE: What a tragic mystery that civil wars are the most savage of all.

GRANT: That's very often true.

MARIE: Finally, as I knew it must, came my family's last night together.

We sat very close that night. The King put his hands, so lovingly, on little Louis' shoulders and instructed him never to think of avenging his father's death.

MORE: (He speaks in a warm tone.) Your Majesty, history now knows that your unfortunate husband was a man without gifts, and largely without charm. We know that your marriage was entered into for reasons of state, and that in the absence of love your heart had, of its own accord, turned to Fersen. And yet now, as you speak of your husband, there is great tenderness and compassion in your voice.

MARIE: Thank you, Sir Thomas.

Yes, Louis and I had, for many years, lived largely separate lives. But I had dutifully borne him four children and, strange to say, at the end, in the last days, we had come finally to live as a family, all of us sharing the same quarters, the same table, and the same emotions that our sufferings gave rise to. When we faced death together, a great fondness for the poor man welled up within me.

Louis was a warm and considerate father, and he had never done me the slightest cruelty. In fact, I was the only woman he ever loved. He was weak, yes, but not evil. Oh, I pitied him and, at the end, I loved him. When it came time, that last night, for His Majesty to retire, I said to him, "Oh, promise us that you will see us again." He took my hand in his. "I will see you in the morning," he said, in his calm way, "before I go." But, after withdrawing, he instructed his servants that we should not be told of the time for his departure. And so it was.

At six o'clock the next morning—it was very dark and cold—the guard from the King's room came up to get His Majesty's prayerbook. In the Tower there was silence, then a few voices in the courtyard.

(She breathes deeply.) At ten o'clock in the morning I heard a frightening roar from the distant crowd . . . and I knew that my husband was dead. *(She falls silent, tearful.)*

MORE: As Her Majesty told us of her sufferings I was deeply moved, but I could not help thinking of the great harm wrought in this world by the members of nation-states. By mobs marching behind a flag.

MARX: *(He too is subdued.)* But Sir Thomas, why should we expect the common people to be any more civilized than the nations to which they belong?

Consider: If a man does not believe that he is bound by any laws, we call that man a criminal. But nations have always acted in such a criminal fashion. A nation will lie, murder, cheat, steal—it will do anything to preserve itself, even though it imprisons its individual citizens for doing exactly the same things.

That was why I preached internationalism, a new order, in which our chief loyalty would be to the brotherhood of man, not just to Germany or Poland or China.

GRANT: Oh, sure, Marx, but you want all that done under communism.

MARX: Damn it, Grant, I know perfectly well that mistakes have been made by my followers. But let me tell you something! Your criticisms of communism may, some of them, be well taken, and yet you must understand that in making them you have done nothing whatever to resolve the serious problems which gave rise to communism! The main problem, of course, is worldwide poverty. Let us suppose that communism, in all its forms, vanished from the face of the earth this very night! *(He snaps his fingers.)* Like that! Tomorrow morning you would awaken to find that more than half the world is still living in poverty and misery! What do you Americans propose to do about that?

GRANT: Well, our foreign aid is certainly a—

MARX: Foreign aid? Are you serious? You give comparatively little to the poor nations, and even that little is given over the objections of a great many of you. Don't you see, foreign aid is no solution at all to the main problem. It's like giving an aspirin to a man suffering from cancer. So after all your diatribes about Communist prison camps and forced labor and the Berlin wall and all of that, you are still faced with the fact that most of the world is hungry and restless!

Do you not perceive that systems are going to have to be changed? Your economic solutions have worked quite well for most, though by no means all, of the people in your great cities. But they have not brought such magical results to the impoverished millions in Asia or Africa or Latin America! That is where a huge part of your problem lies. There and in the slums of your great cities! We Communists think we have a solution. I believe history will prove my solution the proper one, but it is just possible I might have been mistaken. You people have practically no solution. And most of you do not even seem to be aware that there is a problem that cries out for a solution! I tell you this, my friend. Until you offer a real ray of hope to the hungry multitudes of the earth, they will laugh at you when you preach your anti-Communist sermons!

GRANT: Well, now, Marx, whether we have the answer or not, that doesn't make your solution the right one. You tell me this; if communism is so admirable, why, to this day, are millions of people trying to break out of Communist states when nobody at all is trying to break in!!

MARX: But don't you see—

STEVE: Your Majesty, and gentlemen, there's a great deal more ground we should cover this evening. I know Dr. Marx would like to answer that question.

MARX: Indeed!

STEVE: But unfortunately we are out of time. I do hope that you'll be able to join us on our next program to continue this discussion. Will that be possible?

MARX: Certainly, sir. I insist! *(The others all murmur their assent.)*

STEVE: Very well.

When our four distinguished visitors return, Her Majesty will tell us of her trial and death at the hands of the revolutionaries; Karl Marx will, I assume, further discuss his world-shaking theories; General Grant will tell us of his two terms as president; and Sir Thomas More, I trust, will remind us of the drama of Henry VIII.

MARX: Will you also discuss your famous Utopia, Dr. More?

MORE: I shall be glad to, sir.

STEVE: Very well. Thank you all, and good night.

SHOW #4

President Ulysses S. Grant
(JOSEPH EARLEY)

Queen Marie Antoinette
(JAYNE MEADOWS)

Sir Thomas More
(BERNARD BEHRENS)

Dr. Karl Marx
(LEON ASKIN)

&

Steve Allen

Welcome to "Meeting of Minds," starring, once again, four illustrious visitors from history, who will continue their discussion of last week:

From eighteenth-century France—Her Majesty, Queen Marie Antoinette.

From sixteenth-century England—Sir Thomas More.

From nineteenth-century Germany—the founder of modern communism, Karl Marx.

From nineteenth-century America—the eighteenth President of the United States, Ulysses S. Grant.

And now, your host, Steve Allen. *(Steve enters.)*

STEVE: Welcome once again. Our four fascinating visitors from history seem eager to take up where they left off last week. At that time our first guest told us of his long years of failure, followed by his adventures as general of the Union armies in the Civil War. Here again is President Ulysses S. Grant. *(Grant enters.) (Superimpose: Ulysses S. Grant, 1822–1885.)*

STEVE: Welcome, Mr. President.

GRANT: Thank you, Mr. Allen. Good to be back.

STEVE: There's been a great deal of talk, sir, about corruption in political circles in our country recently. Perhaps later you can tell us if there were similar problems during your own two terms.

GRANT: Well, I won't enjoy it, but I'll tell you about it. Also, speaking as a general, there's something I want to ask Her Majesty.

STEVE: You'll have the opportunity in just a moment, Mr. President, because we bring back now the fascinating lady who held us spellbound last week with her personal stories about the French Revolution.

Ladies and Gentlemen, the last queen France ever had, Her Majesty Marie Antoinette. *(Marie Antoinette enters.) (Superimpose: Marie Antoinette, 1755–1793.)*

STEVE: It's a pleasure to see you again, Your Majesty. Is anything wrong?

MARIE: I can't tell you how insulted I am by the choice of music with which I was introduced.

STEVE: What do you mean?

MARIE: It's a crude song from the gutters of Marseilles, sung by the rabble who marched into Paris, thirsting for my blood!

STEVE: Oh, of course. You're absolutely right. Once again, Your

Majesty, I hope you'll forgive our ignorance. *(Marie and Grant exchange greetings as she seats herself.)*

STEVE: Now, what was it you wished to bring to Her Majesty's attention, Mr. President?

GRANT: Well, last week, Your Majesty, you were telling us about Lafayette arriving with twenty thousand troops to protect you when the mob from Paris stormed the palace at Versailles. Now Lafayette was a hero of our American Revolution, and I've always figured he was a pretty fine soldier. I think if I'd been there—in command of twenty thousand troops, that is—I could have gotten you and the King away to safety. How come Lafayette couldn't do it?

MARIE: I am afraid, Mr. President, that King Louis and I are much to blame.

STEVE: How do you mean, Your Majesty?

MARIE: We did not entirely trust Lafayette because he was sympathetic to some of the aims of the revolutionaries. Also, there was great confusion at the time. We didn't even know that a mob was coming from the city at all until my dear friend Count Axel de Fersen arrived breathless on horseback to warn us.

No one even thought to delay the mob by closing the bridge at Sèvres. Louis could not decide whether to flee or to stand his ground. Lafayette, you see, did not arrive till midnight.

After speaking to the National Assembly he came to the King and said, "Sire, I have come to bring you my own head in order to save your Majesty's." But the King had by then decided that he did not wish to leave Versailles.

GRANT: I see.

STEVE: Well, now we'll reintroduce our third guest, the distinguished Lord Chancellor of England under Henry VIII, the "Man for All Seasons," as he's been called, Sir Thomas More. *(Sir Thomas enters.) (Superimpose: Sir Thomas More, 1478–1535.)*

STEVE: Good evening, Sir Thomas.

MORE: Your Majesty. Gentlemen.

MARIE: May I commend you, Sir Thomas, for calling Dr. Marx to account, when last we met, for the atrocious conduct of some of his followers. Obviously you also share my opinion as to the absurdity of his idea of common ownership of property.

MORE: I am sorry to disappoint you, Your Majesty, but in fact I do not.

MARIE: Why, Sir Thomas, you don't mean—

MORE: I'll explain a bit later when, I understand, we'll be discussing my *Utopia*.

STEVE: Yes. And now, our fourth visitor from the pages of history. He published a pamphlet called *The Communist Manifesto* in 1848, and the world is still reeling from the repercussions.

The founder of the most influential mass movement since Christianity: historian, philosopher, Karl Marx. *(Marx enters. Superimpose: Karl Marx, 1818–1883.)*

MARX: Good evening, Your Majesty. Gentlemen.

STEVE: Good evening, Dr. Marx.

MARX: What, no booing this time?

STEVE: Perhaps I should explain to our new viewers that last time when Dr. Marx walked onstage a number of people in the audience expressed their displeasure.

MARX: Their displeasure is understandable, Mr. Allen. Yours is, as you say, a free country. Therefore those who oppose my views are at liberty to make their own opinions known.

But perhaps, for their own benefit, they should learn just what it is that I proposed to the world, no? If they scarcely understand what I say, how can they offer intelligent opposition?

GRANT: Well, now, ya know, Marx, a man doesn't have to understand your entire philosophy to know that he doesn't like the idea of dictatorship. Even if it's called the "dictatorship of the workers."

MARX: You're quite right, Mr. President. Nobody likes dictatorship. It must be tiresome even for the dictators. But nobody "likes" surgery or warfare or any other stern measures. And yet such things are sometimes necessary, for a certain period of time, in order to avoid worse evils.

GRANT: Worse? What's worse than not bein' able to read and write what you want? What's worse than not bein' able to travel where ya want? What's worse than not bein' able to worship where ya want?

MARX: I shall be glad to tell you. Starving to death is worse! Living in lifelong misery and poverty is worse! Slavery is worse!

I'm quite aware that there is a problem in balancing security and freedom.

GRANT: Well, in the U.S.A. we try to give the people some of both.

MARX: Perhaps you should try harder, my friend. But I must clear up yet one more capitalist misconception.

STEVE: And what is that?

MARX: My plan for the dictatorship by the workers was not intended to be a dictatorship in the common meaning of that term. It was supposed to mean rule not by one man, or a small group, but by the majority of the people.

STEVE: Well, now, gentlemen, we'll get back—

MARX: No, wait a moment, sir! Speaking of stern measures, Mr. President, you, as general of the Union armies in the Civil War, you killed thousands of Southerners, and you sacrificed many thousands of your own men in doing so, did you not?

GRANT: Certainly, I did. But war is war.

MARX: Quite so. And dictatorship is dictatorship!

STEVE: Were you criticized for your tactics in battle, Mr. President?

GRANT: Oh, sure. You get criticized in this world no matter what you do. But I won quick victories at Fort Henry and Fort Donelson early in the war, and there's nothing that will silence criticism like winning the game.

MARX: As I understand Mao Tse-tung came to realize.

GRANT: *(He gives Marx a sour look.)* The courage my men showed in these engagements, and the success of my tactics, brought me to the attention of President Lincoln and people in Washington generally; and I was then promoted to major general of the Volunteers.

STEVE: You fought an important battle at Shiloh, didn't you, sir?

GRANT: You're damned right. Our first day there the Confederates surprised us with a heavy attack, and we lost far too many good men. That made me mad! So I rallied our fellows and on the second day we forced the Confederates to withdraw! Again there was criticism.

STEVE: About what?

GRANT: About the heavy loss of life. But Abraham Lincoln stuck up for me. I showed the President that he'd made the right decision by my successful campaign at Vicksburg, Mississippi, in the summer of 1863.

As a result of that victory I was put in command of all the Union troops between the Allegheny Mountains and the Mississippi River.

STEVE: Was it soon after that that you won a really major victory by beating General Brackston Bragg at Chattanooga, Mr. President?

GRANT: That's right. Since I guess I was doing better than any other Union general at that time, I was then placed in top command of the Union armies. You must understand that, up to that time, the Union was gettin' whipped by the South. But Bill Sherman and I put a stop to that!

From the spring of '64 on, things went generally well for the North. General William Sherman was commander in the West, and I handled things in the East, working against General Robert E. Lee in Virginia.

Again I was severely criticized for what some stupid people thought was my indifference to heavy loss of life in the battles of the Wilderness, at Spotsylvania, and at Cold Harbor. But I nevertheless stuck to my basis philosophy of battle.

MORE: And what was that, sir?

GRANT: Never give the enemy a breathing spell! You see, if you give a good fighting man a chance to rest, under the excuse that you need a rest yourself, then you're allowing him to build up his strength and rethink his tactics. That would have been dangerous 'cause the South had better generals than we did.

STEVE: The South had the better generals?

GRANT: Sure! Oh, we had Phil Sheridan, who I consider one of the great commanders of all time, and Sherman. But anyway, my approach was never turn back!

MARIE: Fascinating. Were *all* of your battles instant successes, Mr. Grant?

GRANT: Oh, by no means, Your Majesty. It was very tough going at Spotsylvania, and there was once again heavy loss of life. Lincoln was worried about the way things were going, but I told him that I proposed to fight it out on that line if it took all summer!

When I got to the Richmond area I found that I was unable to break Lee's army in a frontal attack. He was a damned fine soldier. And, incidentally, a fine gentleman.

(He demonstrates with props on the table.) Well, as I say, I couldn't take him head on right at that point, so I crossed around the James River and laid siege to Petersburg. That cut the Southern line of supply, and eventually Lee's troops had to get out of Richmond for that reason.

In the meantime Sherman was marching through Atlanta, and things were falling into place real good.

Finally Robert E. Lee's army surrendered at Appomattox on April 19, 1865, and that was about it.

STEVE: After four long tragic years. So after the war, Mr. Grant, you decided to seek political office?

GRANT: Nope. I was never particularly interested in politics. You can usually tell what a soldier means when he talks, but you can't always say the same thing about a politician.

Anyway, after the war was over there was the problem of how to bring the North and South back together again. Lincoln had wanted to be generous to the South—he was the greatest man I ever knew—but they killed him! That made the job of reconstruction a lot tougher.

MORE: Was slavery the basic issue of your Civil War, Mr. President?

GRANT: No, it wasn't. Oh, slavery was important. But both governments understood that the basic issue was anarchy.

STEVE: Anarchy?

GRANT: Yep. The South called it states' rights. The big question was: Did the Union—the Federal Government, the American majority—have authority over the individual states? I'll tell you this, if this country ever again starts breakin' up into small pieces, I think the cause of freedom will suffer a great blow.

MARX: Speaking of slavery, Mr. President, you realize, of course, that slavery was perpetuated by wealthy American cotton growers for purely economic reasons. Certainly it was atrocious, but perfectly consistent with your economic system.

GRANT: Now see here, Marx. The American people rose up and put a stop to the shame of slavery. Under *your* system people can't rise up to do *anything*!

MARX: Grant, you don't know what you're talking about. There's no need for revolution in a Communist state since the government is—to borrow a phrase from your Mr. Lincoln—of the people, by the people, and for the people.

MORE: You're not denying the role of violence in revolution, are you, Dr. Marx?

MARX: Certainly not. But violence, like force of all kinds, must be applied intelligently. And it means nothing if it is not accompanied by a campaign of education to raise the revolutionary consciousness of a people. But senseless violence by political illiterates is something *I* certainly will not accept the blame for!

STEVE: You might want to communicate that thought to some of our present-day American revolutionaries, Dr. Marx.

MARX: I wish I could. These ignorant young fools with their bombs and guns are the kind of revolutionaries that Vladimir Ilich

Lenin warned against! They are romantic adventurists who give revolution a bad name.

STEVE: I see.

Well, now, Mr. President, despite the early failures you told us about last week, history has identified you as a very competent general. Were you then as successful as a politician?

GRANT: No, I wasn't. Like I told ya, I had never taken any particular interest in politics. In fact, prior to 1868 I had voted only once in a national election, and that time I voted for a Democrat, James Buchanan. Because the North won the war, and because I got more credit for that than I deserved, both parties wanted me to be their candidate. I guess if the South had won, Robert E. Lee would have been elected president. Anyway I went with Lincoln's party, the Republicans.

STEVE: General Eisenhower did the same thing after World War II.

GRANT: Is that right? Well, my old friends and associates were military men, and I had supporters in the business world. I didn't know a great many politicians. So the appointments I made to my first cabinet were mostly personal friends, and also wealthy men who had been helpful to me.

STEVE: That's probably what led to the corruption of your administration.

GRANT: I'm afraid so. People I trusted took advantage of my unfamiliarity with the terrain.

STEVE: What did you do at the end of your second term, Mr. President?

GRANT: Well, now that's a better question than you might think.

STEVE: Oh? Why is that?

GRANT: Well, for a couple of years or so after I left office in 1877, the family and I toured around Europe and the Far East, where we got a mighty nice welcome. I had a great trip through part of China. Fascinating country. Unfortunately after I got back home, in 1881, I was living in New York City, a former two-term president of the United States, and almost flat broke.

MARIE: Why, that's dreadful!

GRANT: Thank you, Your Majesty. I'll tell you something; if it hadn't been for donations from personal friends, this country might have witnessed the fascinating spectacle of a President of the United States going to the poorhouse!

MARIE: Well, I think that's shameful, Mr. President.

GRANT: I'll tell you, though, although the country didn't take too good care of me after I left the White House, they sure did give me a mighty good gravestone.

STEVE: Yes, that famous tomb of yours there in New York City cost about six hundred thousand dollars to build by the time it was dedicated in 1897 by President McKinley. And an interesting thing, Mr. President, is that the American people themselves put up all of that money. Every penny was raised by popular subscription.

GRANT: Yeah. Now, why they couldn't have raised some of that money for me when I was still livin' and needed it, I really don't know.

STEVE: Well, the American people did put your picture on the fifty-dollar bill.

GRANT: That's right. So you might say I'm still in circulation.
But enough about me. I'd like to hear from Sir Thomas.

STEVE: All right.

GRANT: Sir Thomas, will you tell us of your relationship with Henry VIII and about your famous work *Utopia?*

MORE: Gladly, Mr. President.

MARIE: Sir Thomas, did you originate the concept of "utopia"?

MORE: No, indeed, Your Majesty. A number of philosophers over the centuries had explored the idea. Plato's most important dialogue, *The Republic,* includes an outline of an ideal state.

MARX: To me, Sir Thomas, the most interesting argument in your *Utopia* was your criticism of private property.

MARIE: *(She is shocked.)* No, Sir Thomas.

MORE: It is true, Your Majesty. In my Utopia all things were held in common. For I believe that the public good cannot flourish where men hold important property in private. There's no question but that I did indeed advocate a form of communism, although I saw it as a form which men should freely choose rather than something imposed on them by *force. (He gives Marx a look.)*

MARX: I so saw it myself, if we are talking about a majority.

MARIE: What did you suggest, Sir Thomas, about people becoming attached to the property they used, whether they owned it or not?

MORE: In my Utopia, Your Majesty, the people changed houses every ten years to prevent their becoming too attached to any one place and its artifacts.

MARIE: How amusing. Like musical chairs.

STEVE: The Utopians' treatment of crime and punishment was

considered revolutionary at the time, wasn't it, Sir Thomas?

MORE: Yes. The Utopians thought it absolute folly to make the death penalty common punishment for *all* crimes ranging from theft to murder. This was quite revolutionary for as late as 1800—some 300 years after my Utopia—England still had some 230 offenses punishable by hanging!

STEVE: What was life like in the cities of Utopia?

MORE: Well, the cities and towns were kept small, and if a town grew too large, some of the inhabitants were to be moved to another location.

STEVE: You may be the first man who thought of busing.

GRANT: What would you do in these small towns to amuse yourself? Was there hunting or—?

MORE: No, Mr. President, the killing of beasts for food was done by *specialists*. This you understand, would rule out hunting, which is cruel, even when done solely for the purpose of gathering food. When it is done purely for what men call sport, it is a degrading and barbaric spectacle.

As if men had the right to *amuse* themselves by killing defenseless animals.

STEVE: What about eating habits in Utopia?

MORE: Eating at home was permitted, but most people would prefer to eat in common dining rooms, to enjoy each other's company, as was done in the monasteries, or by Christ and his Apostles.

MARIE: How friendly.

MARX: And how communistic.

STEVE: Tell us about the educational system in your Utopia.

MORE: Learning was open to all, without distinction of sex.

MARIE: Really?

MORE: Yes, Your Majesty, and indeed, in reality, my three daughters were very well educated and constantly encouraged. That is, after their normal and necessary duties as wives and mothers were attended to. I advised them never to neglect their husbands but rather that they should be a constant source of inspiration to them.

STEVE: We'll no doubt hear a rebuttal from some women's libbers on one of our future discussions. Perhaps when Susan B. Anthony joins us.

GRANT: What was considered the strangest recommendation from your Utopia, Sir Thomas?

MORE: Perhaps, Mr. President, it was the idea that if a patient had an extremely painful and incurable disease, he would be permitted, with permission of the magistrate and priest, to end his own life, if he wished.

STEVE: Well now, I'm puzzled, Sir Thomas. You are, quite understandably, a hero in the Catholic tradition. Indeed a saint. Isn't suicide a *sin* in the context of Catholic morality?

MORE: Unquestionably. However you must remember you asked me to speak of my Utopia, which was a fictional land full of virtuous pagans. The Utopians were not Christians.

(All are amused.)

STEVE: I see. What would you consider your basic teaching?

MORE: My most important teaching—both in my Utopia and in my actual life—was of the evil of private property.

GRANT: Evil, you say?

MORE: Yes, both economically and morally. For without private property, Mr. President, the vices of greed and pride would have very little to feed on; and the worst of all sins is *pride*.

In any event, the intention of my *Utopia* was not so much to depict an ideal society as to censure some aspects and evils of existing society.

And my dear friend Erasmus said, "If you have not read More's *Utopia*, do look for it when you wish to be amused."

MARIE: Well now, one thing that bothers me about your Utopia, Sir Thomas, and for that matter, about your Utopia, Dr. Marx, is that life in one or the other would be indescribably boring.

GRANT: I agree.

MARIE: You gentlemen overlook the fact that people are just naturally different in their tastes.

GRANT: That's right, Your Majesty.

But your greatness, Sir Thomas, if you will permit me, comes out of your behavior when provoked by Henry VIII.

STEVE: Yes, let's narrow in on that area, if we may? Where were you educated, Sir Thomas?

MORE: Partly at Oxford, sir. For a time I was attracted to the priesthood, but my dear friend Erasmus thought I would be better suited for the law.

GRANT: Were you married, Sir Thomas?

MORE: With three daughters? Very much so.

GRANT: Oh, yes. I forgot.

MORE: In 1505 I took to wife the beautiful, kind, and generous Jane

Colt, who bore me three daughters and a son. As I say, I had been attracted to the priesthood but decided it was better to become a faithful husband rather than an *un*faithful priest.

STEVE: When did you first enter the King's service?

MORE: I became the King's counsel in 1518. I had declined the honor several times but accepted after a talk with Henry in which he said, "Look first upon God and next upon your King." He was aware that the mainspring of my life was my religious faith.

MARIE: Did you often visit the King's palace?

MORE: No, Your Majesty. The King frequently invited me; but the way of life there did not appeal to me, so I declined his invitations, gracefully, of course. He came to my house in Chelsea several times . . . uninvited. We dined and he loved to walk with me in my garden, his arm about my shoulder, pondering all sorts of things.

STEVE: When did you become chancellor?

MORE: In 1529 after Henry deprived Cardinal Wolsey of "The Great Seal."

MARX: We can measure Sir Thomas's virtue by contrasting his behavior in office with that of Cardinal Wolsey. Wolsey's income would be the equivalent today of millions of dollars each year.

Yes. And his *palaces* actually surpassed the King's in grandeur. For fourteen years—although he acted in the King's name—he, Wolsey, was, in effect, ruler of all England.

GRANT: Incredible. But what sort of fellow was Henry VIII?

MORE: It might surprise many in the modern day to know that if his elder brother, Prince Arthur, had not died, Henry would have held office in the Church. His father had seen to it that he was very well educated. He studied Latin, French, Italian, music, theology. And he was a great sportsman.

STEVE: Were there any early signs of Protestant or rebellious tendencies?

MORE: Oh, not at all. So devoted was he to the Catholic faith that he heard five masses on important holy days, and frequently three on other days. He even assisted the priest at mass personally. His fervent contributions in theological controversy earned him from the Pope the title of "Defender of the Faith." He had declared very strongly, you see, against that rebellious troublemaker Martin Luther.

STEVE: That remark, Sir Thomas, means we'll now have to offer Luther equal time.

MORE: *(He laughs heartily.)* I should like to be here when you do.

Henry's virtues were many, but he had a violent temper and could never respond to opposition gracefully. During his thirty-eight years on the throne, many a subject felt the crunch of his royal heel.

MARX: To put it mildly.

STEVE: Can you tell us the story, Sir Thomas, of what led to the conflict between King Henry and yourself?

MORE: Yes. In 1509 when he was only a boy of eighteen Henry had married his brother Arthur's widow, Princess Catherine of Aragon. She was, as you know, the daughter of Ferdinand and Isabella of Spain, known chiefly to American schoolchildren, I suppose, as the monarchs who despatched Columbus to the New World.

MARX: And to historians as the monarchs who banished the Jews from Spain.

MORE: Alas, yes. Well, for twenty-two long years Catherine's role as Henry's wife was undisputed. She gave birth to a daughter, Mary, but as Henry waited—not very patiently, I'm afraid—for an heir, one child after another was born dead.

Then Henry became infatuated with Anne Boleyn and wished to make her more than his mistress. He wished, in fact, to make her his queen. Henry sent an emissary to the Pope, Clement VII, to seek an annulment of his marriage to Catherine.

When this failed, Wolsey and Dr. Thomas Cranmer, acting on Henry's behalf, sought to prove that his marriage to Catherine had never been legal because she had previously been married to his brother.

GRANT: What's that got to do with it?

MORE: Perhaps very little. But we lawyers are paid to clutch at straws when necessary. But, quite seriously, there was some legal weight to Henry's argument, though I was not persuaded.

In 1531 Henry became aware that he risked excommunication if he persisted on his course. Henry managed to force through Parliament a bill stipulating that if the Pope should indeed make good any such threats, then the king, Henry, would become supreme head of the Church in England.

At that my conscience forced me to resign as lord chancellor.

In January of 1533 Henry committed bigamy by marrying Anne Boleyn; and in July the Pope formally threatened excommunication, declaring the marriage invalid.

Henry's personal fate thereafter became increasingly tragic. He was so disappointed when Anne Boleyn gave birth to a daughter, Elizabeth, that he refused to even look at the infant and became involved with Sir John Seymour's daughter, Jane.

Henry's response to opposition at this period was particularly brutal. Hundreds were drawn and quartered, disemboweled, or hanged, simply because they remained loyal to the only Church they had ever known.

STEVE: Incredible.

MARX: Well, now, there was somewhat more to it than that. Many of those hanged were in a state of armed rebellion, and they also were then quite prepared to accept help from an enemy country, Spain, simply because it was Catholic.

And in Henry's defense, Sir Thomas, it should be pointed out that by comparison to the atrocities that were committed only a few decades thereafter on the continent of Europe, King Henry's version of the Reformation seems almost appealing.

Elizabeth I, you know, had some three hundred Catholics executed as traitors.

But you have explained to us earlier, Sir Thomas, your sensitive awareness of the faults, the cruelty and corruption, of the Church in that day. And yet you remained loyal to it. Why?

MORE: It seemed to me, Dr. Marx, an institution well worth preserving. It needed to be purified, yes, but not destroyed.

When Henry at last perceived that my highest loyalty was to God, and not to Caesar, I was beheaded.

STEVE: The charge?

MORE: Failure to acknowledge the King's supremacy over the Church.

MARX: Your fellow monarch, Your Majesty, again showed the level of his personal degree of civilization by publicly exhibiting Sir Thomas's head on London Bridge.

MARIE: How monstrous.

MARX: But, of course, churchmen on *all* sides in that day thought that capital punishment was perfectly suitable for their opponents.

And I'm sure, Sir Thomas, that you would not want those listening to acquire the impression that you were some sort of heroic defender of freedom of thought or conscience. Were you

not yourself one of the leading heresy hunters of your day? Had
you not criticized Luther in the strongest possible terms.

MORE: Yes, of course, of course.

STEVE: Thank you, Sir Thomas.

Now Your Majesty, if you'll forgive me, the world never
knew about your romance with Count Axel de Fersen until
about a hundred years after his death, when your love letters to
him were found in a vault kept by members of his family in
Sweden.

Do you think the fact that the French people knew nothing
about Count de Fersen—but obviously knew that you weren't
in love with your husband—do you suppose that could have
led to the gossip that you were, as they called you, a loose
woman?

MARIE: *(She is on guard.)* Yes, I believe so, but I do not wish to
discuss the matter.

MORE: Mr. Allen, may I suggest that we respect Her Majesty's
wishes in this most private matter?

MARIE: No. Thank you, Sir Thomas. It's all right. I must defend
Fersen's honor. The Count de Fersen, sir, proved a courageous
and reliable friend, to all of our family, in our moments of
greatest danger.

At great risk to himself—when there was a price on his
head—he tried to help us escape.

MARX: Your Majesty, we know now that you brought many of
your troubles on yourself. Isn't it quite possible that things
would have gone better for you if you had not tried to escape?

MARIE: Dr. Marx, are you saying that *I* was responsible for the
vicious reprisals the revolutionaries inflicted on me? You had
children, sir?

MARX: *(He frowns, pauses.)* Yes.

MARIE: Then your heart must have bled for them, as you say it did
for the poor. Well, let me tell you. After the failure of my
second escape plan, in order to punish me the authorities took
my son, the Dauphin, from me.

They said they were doing it because they wanted to educate
him properly, but they put him under the care of a tutor,
Simon, a shoemaker, who was illiterate, the plan being to raise
him as one of the lowest class rather than in the station to which
he had been born.

I pleaded with them. I said, "You would do better to kill me
than to take my son away."

Do you know, I was forbidden to visit him, even when he was taken ill. However I did discover one day a little opening in the spiral staircase. You know, Sir Thomas, how in prisons they have those little slits in the stone wall to let the light in?

MORE: Only too well, Your Majesty.

MARIE: Well, there I would stand by the hour, waiting for him to come out in the courtyard to play so I could catch a glimpse of him. But it didn't take him long to forget who he was; and I would stand there, with the tears running down my face, watching my son wearing the red cap of the *revolutionists* and singing that dreadful song you were playing when I came out here this evening. You know now why it upset me so.

STEVE: Yes, of course. I'm sorry.

MARIE: Finally the day came when they moved me from the Temple to le Conciergerie. I was put in a cell as narrow, damp, and dark as a coffin. It was in the basement, and the already grated window was even bricked halfway up. There was practically no air. I wasn't even allowed a candle. In fact, the only light I had came from an oil lamp down the hall.

They took everything from me. The watch my mother had given me before I left Austria as a girl. They even took away my handkerchief. All I had left was an iron bed and a stool. (*She weeps, openly.*)

MARX: (*He speaks gently, for the first time.*) Your Majesty, your account of your sufferings in that cell is truly touching. But did you know who built such cells, and such prisons? It was the royalty. Had you ever before given so much as a thought to the thousands who had suffered in such cells?

Had you ever pitied the destitute, the forgotten, even the innocent, who had languished in your prisons?

MORE: Dr. Marx, the moment is not appropriate.

MARX: Perhaps you are right. Excuse me.

MARIE: Nine months after my husband's death, hemorrhaging severely, weak from lack of air and exercise, I was brought to trial.

MORE: It is said that during the trial, Your Majesty, you showed yourself to be the true queen you had failed to be in the glittering Court of Versailles.

MARIE: Tribulation, gentlemen, first makes one realize what one is.

At my trial, since not one witness could produce a shred of incriminating evidence against me as *queen*, they uttered the most flagrant untruths to convict me as a *woman*.

STEVE: What do you mean, Your Majesty?

MARIE: I . . . my eight-year-old son was called as the first witness. Against me.

GRANT: No.

MARIE: Yes, gentlemen, the Dauphin was put on the stand. I can still see him seated in a big armchair, swinging his little legs. His feet didn't reach the floor, you see.

But they had frightened him and poisoned his mind. And here, in front of all those strangers, they asked if it were true that his mother had had . . . *sexual relations* with him. He even clung to the foul lies they had taught him when his outraged sister confronted him with the truth!

When asked to respond, I said, "If I have made no reply it is because nature itself refuses to answer such a charge. I appeal in this matter to all the mothers present in the court."

There was a hush. . . . I could see the women were profoundly affected, and it is interesting, I think, that later, when I was sentenced, this charge was dropped.

But my death had long since been decided upon. At last, on October 16, 1793, I removed my faded black and replaced it with a pure white muslin gown. I covered my head with nothing more than a simple linen cap. Sampson, the executioner, cut my hair, bound my hands, and I was led out like an animal, on a rope, into the cart, to be paraded before the howling mob.

But the savage noises of the streets didn't make any impression on me, nor did the savage sights. The bitterness of death had already passed. I had died, you see, four days earlier when my son had denied me in the courtroom.

MORE: Your Majesty, whatever became of the Dauphin?

MARIE: I wish I knew, Sir Thomas. That is one of the great mysteries of history. Whether like Count de Fersen and my husband, the King, he was murdered, I know not. I only hope he didn't suffer.

MARX: It is a deep question, is it not, Sir Thomas, as to why every large human achievement seems to come wrapped in tragedy.

MORE: One's faith must be very strong indeed to perceive the workings of Divine Providence in the blood-spattered record of human progress. (*There is a pause.*)

STEVE: Well, now, Dr. Marx, we've heard at length—both on

your last visit and this evening—from everyone but yourself.
May we put some personal questions to you?

MARX: *(He is still lost in thought, but then responds.)* Oh? But of course.

STEVE: In what year were you born?

MARX: In 1818, sir, in the town of Trier, in the German Rhineland.
My people were German Jews who had converted to Christianity.

MORE: What about your education?

MARX: Well, my father was a lawyer and fortunately tutored me in
the works of such Enlightenment thinkers as Voltaire, John
Locke, and Diderot.

As a young student at the University of Berlin I encountered
the teachings of Feuerbach and the renowned philosopher
Hegel.

Hegel, you know, saw all of history as a series of conflicts in
which the old order, which we may call *thesis*, is challenged by a
new force, *antithesis*, and ultimately resolves into a different
system, a *synthesis*, or combination, of the earlier two.

It occurred to me when I was studying Hegel, that this
simple idea could also be applied to the conflict between the
workers and the upper classes. I foresaw the final synthesis as a
classless utopia that would follow a Communist revolution.

When I was twenty-two, I declared war on the Prussian
government.

GRANT: *(He chuckles.)* What were your demands?

MARX: I called for an end of all official controls over newspaper
publications, for one thing.

MORE: Dr. Marx, are you familiar with the degree of control over
the press today in Communist countries?

MARX: Not intimately, Sir Thomas. But I am familiar with the
degree of official control over the press in Catholic countries,
down through the centuries.

MORE: But my dear sir, I am quite prepared to concede that the
Church was mistaken in those cases. I wonder when *your*
followers will be prepared to make the same concession!

STEVE: Where did you meet Friedrich Engels, Dr. Marx?

MARX: I met him in Paris. He was a fascinating fellow, the son of a
German cotton manufacturer, and perhaps the best educated
man in Europe. He was very useful to me, because for one thing
he had learned the ugly realities of industrial tyranny while
working in a branch of his father's firm at Manchester,
England.

Infuriated by what he discovered, he wrote a booklet titled
The Condition of the Working Class in England, a scathing indict-
ment of the capitalist system.

STEVE: Engels gave you a great deal of financial support over the
years, did he not?

MARX: He did, sir.

(*He smiles.*) You know, it's funny, Engels took the profits
piled up by his father's manufacturing enterprise and used that
money to finance social revolution throughout Europe.

GRANT: Just what was it, Dr. Marx, that you had against the upper
classes?

MARX: The upper classes, Mr. President? That is to say the nobility, the aristocracy? They were, if I may be frank, not of much
interest to me. I saw them as falling naturally from the tree of
history and unlikely to be replaced. It was the *bourgeoisie*, the
money-grubbing middle class, that I saw as the chief danger to
the interests of the poor workers.

Anyway, I recommended that the workers seize power and
destroy the concept of individual property. I naturally foresaw
that a few would suffer; but since the overwhelming majority
were the poor workers and peasants, it followed that the great
majority would benefit under my system. Which is better for a
society, I ask you, that the 10 percent suffer or that the 90
percent suffer?

I closed my argument in *The Communist Manifesto* with these
words, "The ruling classes tremble at a Communistic Revolution. The proletarians, the workers, have nothing to lose but
their chains. They have a world to win. *Proletarier aller lander
vereinigt euch.* Working men of all countries, unite!"

MORE: Your efforts were not immediately successful, were they,
Marx?

MARX: No, Sir Thomas. There were seemingly endless years of
struggle, dissension.

Taking advantage of the uprisings and troubles in Germany
in 1848—the year of your California Gold Rush, Mr. Grant—
I moved the headquarters of the Communist League to Co-
logne, but my work there failed.

I was forced to flee to Paris. But there, too, the right wing
was becoming dominant, so I ran to England.

STEVE: Those were particularly dark days for you, weren't they?

MARX: Yes, I lived in two rooms on Bloom Street in Soho, a
rundown section of London. In these disease-ridden surround-

ings, Your Majesty, three of my children died.

MARIE: *(She reacts sympathetically.)*

MARX: Can you imagine the anguish and fury I felt? This unhappiness only added fuel to the fires that burned in me. I spent most of my waking hours in the British Museum studying and writing, reading about the disgraceful conditions in England's mines and factories. It was in these years, Your Majesty, that I wrote my now-famous attack on capitalism, *Das Kapital*. I had to let the world know that individual human beings, innocent men, women, and children, were being *brutalized*, treated like *animals*, paid just a few pennies to do back-breaking labor, ruining their health, being injured and killed. Perhaps some men can stand idly by at the contemplation of such suffering, but I could not.

MORE: It is one of the great tragedies of modern history, my friends, that we Christians of Europe simply accepted all the terrible suffering of those days as part of the natural order. Our hearts did not bleed for the impoverished and exploited working people as they should have.

And because of our hardness of heart, Dr. Marx and the Communists who followed him were able to say to the workers, "You see, no one in the established order cares about you. The royalty does not care about you. The aristocracy, the nobility do not care about you. And the Church offers you prayer, which you cannot trade in at the store for food or clothing for your children."

GRANT: I never thought any of this through before, Sir Thomas, but now that I hear you lay it out like that it seems to me you're right. The rest of us should have done more for the poor than we did, I guess. But remember, our American economic system did give millions of people good jobs and a sense of hope for the future.

MORE: Yes, that's true, Mr. President.

(To Marx.) Were you interested in reforming the conditions of English workers?

MARX: Not really, Sir Thomas. I wanted revolution, not reform.

GRANT: Was it your opinion, Marx, that capitalism was totally evil?

MARX: On the contrary, I stated in my *Manifesto* that the capitalists were the greatest revolutionaries of their time.

STEVE: Really?

MARX: Yes! Capitalism was the first to show what man's activity can bring about. It accomplished wonders far surpassing the Egyptian pyramids, the Roman aqueducts, and the Gothic cathedrals.

GRANT: Well, since you paid capitalism so many compliments, Marx, perhaps you'll tell us in what respect you disapproved of it.

MARX: Gladly. Let me ask you, Your Majesty, suppose a man's shirt sells for ten dollars. What gives it that value?

MARIE: *(She is perplexed.)* Well, I suppose it would be first the cost of the material of which the shirt is made, plus the cost of the labor required to make it?

MARX: Very good, Your Majesty. You are correct about the value of the labor. Let us say it comes to three dollars. But what is it, in turn, that establishes the cost of the raw material—the cotton, the wool, or silk—which we might decide is two dollars? It is again the value of the labor expended in producing these materials.

But we know that the capitalist who sells the shirt takes care to make a profit, in this case, let us say, of five dollars. Then where does that profit come from? It comes from *surplus value*. The capitalist got more labor than he paid for. In a sense he "stole" that labor from the worker.

GRANT: Oh, now, see here—

MARX: I do *not* argue that the capitalist is consciously a thief. The point is that stealing, taking advantage of others, is an essential element of a system where it's every-man-for-himself. Would you join me, Sir Thomas, in agreeing that there is a serious ethical problem here?

MORE: Absolutely, Dr. Marx. The Christian philosophers of the late Middle Ages produced a very detailed theory designed to guide Christians involved in production and trade. This theory was based on the simple assumption that business conducted only for the sake of profit is essentially immoral. The Church then argued that a man had a right to nothing more than reasonable wages or payment for the services he rendered society.

MARX: And what about the merchant who got rich by taking advantage of his customers and workers?

MORE: The Church insisted that he was no better than a common thief.

MARX: Precisely, Sir Thomas. And would you be good enough to inform Her Majesty what the Church had to say about *usury*.

MORE: Yes. The Church regarded the charging of exorbitant interest on loans as a damnable practice. Usury is also condemned in the Scriptures.

And I understand one of your modern poets, Ezra Pound, held the same opinion.

GRANT: Since the Church doesn't seem to feel that way about high rates of interest today, Sir Thomas, when did the shift in opinion take place?

MORE: It started at the end of the Renaissance period, Mr. Grant. One of the reasons for the Protestant Reformation, you see, was that the new middle class—many of them merchants and shopkeepers—came to realize that their economic interests were in direct conflict with the spiritual ideals of medieval Christianity.

Generally in history, when this sort of pattern emerges, man gradually changes his philosophy so that it will permit him to do what he wants to do for purely selfish motives.

MARX: A fascinating sidelight on this matter, Mr. President, is that it was easy for the Church to look down on moneylenders and bankers during the Middle Ages because at that time many of those engaged in such trades were Jews and Moslems. Therefore the Christians could feel morally superior to these nonbelievers. But once the Christians themselves began accumulating great wealth and controlling banks, then, of course—as Sir Thomas has told us—they began to talk out of the other side of their mouths.

MORE: *(He pauses.)* Dr. Marx, is there anything about the present human condition that comes as a surprise to you?

MARX: Oh, indeed, Sir Thomas. For one thing I am astonished that so many millions of people are still attached to religion.

STEVE: Oh? Why are you astonished?

MARX: Because to me it seemed that reason and true scientific education, on the one hand, were utterly incompatible with religious superstition, on the other. Apparently there was more to the situation than met my eye.

MORE: So it would seem.

STEVE: Does it come as a surprise to you to see that the capitalist economy is still dominant in so many parts of the earth?

MARX: In a way, yes. A hundred years have passed since I predicted the collapse of capitalism. And yet the collapse obviously has not taken place. But do not pride yourselves, my friends, on your great moral superiority, for as I look at your society today it does not seem to me that you have any. The revolutionary ideals expressed by your founding fathers—Jefferson, Benjamin Franklin, Thomas Paine, and others—these inspired many people, at the beginning of your country's history, to a historic sense of mission.

And yet see what has come of your social experiment, in a short two hundred years! Millions in your society have a sense of being lost in the world, unsure of themselves and their future. Millions are addicted to narcotics, to alcohol. The family in your society is disintegrating, and millions suffer from emotional distress. Pornography is everywhere, the poor of your large cities become even more desperate. No, no, my friends, while your system has not as yet collapsed, I think it would be very rash to place a large wager on its long-term survival.

STEVE: Well now, just a minute, Dr. Marx. Weren't you mistaken in assuming that the poor in capitalist countries would grow steadily poorer?

MARX: Yes, I was mistaken, to some extent, but not totally. Many formerly poor people, I observe, have come to *share* in the wealth created by your capitalistic economy.

Oh . . . one of the most surprising things to me is that today my most devoted followers are not always the workers of the Western nations, as I had assumed would be the case, but certain of the intellectuals.

MARIE: Yes, that is odd.

MARX: Most of the workers, I'm sorry to observe, in the United States at least, are staunch defenders of the status quo, and indeed often find themselves opposed to the poor.

MARIE: Did you ever actually say, citizen Marx, that religion is the opiate of the people?

MARX: Yes, citizen Marie. The phrase comes from my *Introduction to a Critique of Hegel's Philosophy of Law*. Hegel, you know, was very religious. But this observation has been misinterpreted by many.

MARIE: Would you then explain it to us?

MARX: With pleasure. There is a legitimate medical use, after all, for derivatives of opium. They kill pain, and they make the reality about us more palatable than it otherwise would be. What I actually said was this. "Religion is the *sigh* of the oppressed creature, the *kindliness* of a *heartless* world, the *soul* of soulless circumstance." In that sense, you see, religion *is* the opiate of the people.

By that I meant that it is a device that enables people to dull the pain of their otherwise frequently painful existence. I regarded religion not so much as a practical evil but rather as something that enabled man to sustain his illusions.

MORE: And did you perceive these "illusions" as always harmful?

MARX: For the most part, yes, Sir Thomas. I believe that man should be *dis*illusioned, so that he may think, act, and shape the world according to his reason.

MORE: Would you deny the common people such comfort?

MARX: Only with considerable reluctance, my friend. My sympathies, you will recall, were always with the common people, with the oppressed, with the workers of the world. I pitied them, because of their poverty, their suffering, their pain, their ignorance, their alienation.

I grant you that religion brought some comfort in their misery, but unfortunately it also discouraged them from rising up, throwing off their chains, and improving their lot. In that sense, I repeat, I considered it an opiate.

STEVE: You know, Dr. Marx, one of the fascinating lessons to emerge from history since your death is that it has apparently been possible for people who still believe in religion nevertheless to support revolutions and to throw off the chains of those who oppress them. There are the Christian Socialists, for example.

MARIE: Is there any one simple idea, Dr. Marx, that you would call a cornerstone of your teachings? I'm afraid that it would have to be simple, if I were to grasp it.

MARX: You do yourself an injustice, Your Majesty. Well, my basic idea is that the general flow of history is determined not so much by religion or military adventures, but rather by economic considerations.

MARIE: Economic?

MARX: Yes. The Industrial Revolution, for example, brought us democracy. It introduced the decline of religious power and greatly changed moral standards. It encouraged scientific development. It affected literature, the arts. It affected the position of women in the world.

And no matter what point in history we consider, you can see these same patterns at work. It was the enormous riches of Cleopatra's Egypt that reinvigorated the Rome of Augustus Caesar. Consider the Crusades, which you teach your children were fought purely for religious reasons. Nonsense. Many of the Knights of Europe who marched to the East were passionately interested in establishing trade routes to the Orient.

Sir Thomas has earlier mentioned the glories of the Renaissance. Many of them would not have come about had it not been for the banking house of the Medici and other wealthy members of the Italian aristocracy.

And the French Revolution would never have been possible had not the middle class, the bourgeoisie, risen to economic power in France. They needed freedom, elbow room, in which to conduct their trade and enterprise. The freedom they sought and obtained helped make way for the Revolution that toppled the French monarchy.

GRANT: Well, you make out a very able case for yourself, Marx. But when we consider the terrible sufferings of so many millions of people in the conflict between East and West since your day I, for one, wish you had never invented socialism.

MORE: Dr. Marx must plead not guilty to that charge, Mr. President. Socialism, in various forms, has been with us for thousands of years. And we must understand that it seems always to have arisen in response to the evils that result when men are motivated only by their own economic self-interest.

MARIE: Yes, but the Church has always been opposed to socialism.

MORE: Oh, no, Your Majesty. Not always. In the seventeenth century the Jesuits in the Portuguese colony of Uruguay organized hundreds of thousands of Indians according to strictly socialistic principles. And in the Protestant Reformation, in Germany, the leader of the peasant rebellion Thomas—

MARX: Thomas Munzer.

MORE: Yes. He urged the people to overthrow the existing government and establish a simple, godly society in which all things were to be owned in common.

STEVE: And in China a century ago the T'ai P'ing Rebellion was led by Christian converts who had certain socialistic ideas.

MORE: And, of course, we know that even Christ and his followers, the Apostles, lived in part a communal existence. In the Acts of the Apostles, chapter IV, verses 34 and 35, we read, "As many as were owners of lands and houses sold them and brought the price of the things they sold, and laid it down before the feet of the Apostles. And distribution was made to *everyone as he had need*."

But it is when socialism denies the importance of God—or indeed the existence of God—that the Church must oppose it.

Speaking from the moral point of view, it is obvious that there is nothing inherently evil whatever in the idea of communal living, people deciding to live together, to give up their individual claims on private property, having the community retain ownership.

STEVE: Many young people in our Jesus movement today do exactly that.

MORE: Certainly it would be a better world if men with untold millions would share their incredible wealth with others less fortunate than themselves. But now, Dr. Marx, let us consider a moral question of enormous importance.

MARX: Which is?

MORE: How justified are the *means* of bringing about the Communist society, and how justified are the means for continuing a Communist dictatorship in power, in the face of popular opposition to it?

MARX: Now see here, More—

MORE: I am speaking, sir. The influential and revolutionary French thinkers we have been mentioning—Rousseau, Voltaire, Montaigne—along with English philosophers such as John Locke, John Stuart Mill, they also, sir, formulated theories on the importance of freedom: the freedom to travel as one might wish, to speak one's mind, to publish one's opinions.

GRANT: Right! The founding philosophers on the American continent—Jefferson, Adams, Franklin, and the rest—they thrilled all mankind when they asserted these freedoms in their Declaration of Independence and in the Constitution of the United States.

MARX: But what you have neglected to mention, gentlemen, is that certain unscrupulous merchants and manufacturers abused that freedom! Why, the American people themselves insisted that such abuses had to be stopped! Your labor unions, your consumer and ecology movements today, continue that fight!

MORE: True, but we turn again to the most important moral question: How do we recognize the point at which in improving the economic plight of the poor we begin to deprive them of their liberties?

MARX: Now, listen, More, it is all well and good to say that government ought not to interfere with business, but this high-sounding abstraction has been used by capitalists as a weapon to defeat every humane act of legislation to benefit the poor that has ever been introduced!

(To audience.) Listen to me, people! Think! Would you like to turn the clock back! Would you want your children to work again in filthy, dangerous factories for twelve or fourteen hours every day, having their bodies crippled and stunted, their spirits broken? Of course not! And yet when the Child Labor Act was first debated, the advocates of capitalism revealed where their sympathies lay: *not* with the oppressed children but with the wealthy factory owners! This, too, was a moral question, Sir Thomas!

MORE: Indeed. I would not defend a single one of the scandalous abuses perpetrated by the powerful, in any age. But would you, sir, defend the atrocities committed in Russia, in China, and in other nations where your philosophy is now dominant? I'm even willing to leave out of our consideration crimes and murders committed in the first flush of a revolution, when—as Her Majesty's descriptions have reminded us—all the participants seem to go mad and terror is the order of the day. This is all horrible enough, but perhaps men may be forgiven such crimes on the grounds that they know not what they do and have been driven to desperation and revenge by the long cruelty of their oppressors.

But let us now consider, sir, those long-continued atrocities and crimes committed not in *hot* but *in cold blood*. Surely in this case the perpetrators know very well what they do. They resort to the firing squad, the slave labor camp, the political prison, not in the momentary heat of anger but as a result of a cold, calculated, systematic plan. It is this, sir, I submit, that in the long run history will not countenance!

MARX: And I submit to you that every government around the globe acts ruthlessly against enemies from without and from within!

MORE: Quite probably, sir; but in each case such resort was still morally disgraceful. But let us be very specific here. It is understandable that a state would choose to defend itself against armed attack by another people. But in some Marxist lands today—as you must observe to your deep sorrow—men are imprisoned, executed, terrorized, not because they approach the seats of power with bombs or plans for armed insurrection but merely because they paint a picture or write a poem or hold a scientific belief or say a casual word to a friend that runs counter to the dominant philosophy.

Such things were all too common in the Dark Ages, during the Inquisition and at other times.

MARX: Including your own time! You did what you could to deny freedom of expression to Luther's followers!

MORE: All right! Agreed. But have we traveled such a long and painful road through history only to learn that our path has been circular and that we are back in the days of the torture rack, the dungeon, and the execution chamber?

MARX: Sir Thomas, I demand that—

STEVE: Gentlemen, please! Unfortunately we have run out of time. Your Majesty, gentlemen, we thank you for an unusually stimulating discussion. I know there were many important points we didn't have time to bring up, but perhaps you'll be able to visit us again.

ALL: *(Murmur assent.)*

SHOW #5

Charles Darwin
(MURRAY MATHESON)

Emily Dickinson
(KATHERINE HELMOND)

Galileo Galilei
(ALEXANDER SCOURBY)

Attila the Hun
(KHIGH DHIEGH)

&

Steve Allen

Welcome again to "Meeting of Minds," which tonight brings you:

From fifth-century Europe—Attila the Hun.

From sixteenth-century Italy—Galileo Galilei.

From nineteenth-century America—poet Emily Dickinson.

From nineteenth-century England, the man who gave us the theory of evolution—Dr. Charles Darwin.

And now your host, Steve Allen.

STEVE: Hello again. First we will meet one of the important figures of scientific history. Like those of Galileo, his theories not only disturbed the world but changed it profoundly. The famous ornithologist James Fisher, commenting on the work of Charles Darwin, has said, "No subsequent synthesis of thought—not even the theory of relativity—has so humbled man, so purged his self-consciousness, so tempered his purpose, and so blessed his wisdom."

Charles Darwin was born in England in 1809. Here is the remarkable Dr. Charles Darwin.

STEVE: Welcome, Dr. Darwin.

(Darwin enters.) (Superimpose: Charles Darwin 1809–1882.)

DARWIN: Thank you, Mr. Allen. I'm delighted to be here, not only to enjoy your invited distinguished company but particularly to visit an age, and a place, where my theories about evolution have long been peacefully accepted. It was quite otherwise in my own time, I assure you.

STEVE: Well, sir, as a matter of fact, it was quite otherwise among many people until fairly recently. Believe it or not, there are even a few today who resist many of the established truths of science, not only your theories.

DARWIN: Really?

STEVE: Yes.

DARWIN: Let us pray for them.

STEVE: Would it be true, Dr. Darwin, to say that you were the first man to develop a theory of evolution?

DARWIN: Oh, not at all sir. You see, behind the theory of evolution is the basically simple notion that God did not invent the hundreds of thousands of animal species by a separate series of magical tricks, or spiritual sleight of hand, but rather that all living things share a common descent.

STEVE: In other words, God didn't invent the tigers one day, the giraffes another day, and the kangaroo some other afternoon.

DARWIN: Precisely. Now this idea had been held by a number of people before my birth. My own grandfather, by the way, Erasmus Darwin, had given some thought to the concept of "natural selection," which I shall explain later. What we are really dealing with here, you see, is another of those ideas whose time has come. I'm sure that had I never been born the theory would have been just as adequately developed by others.

STEVE: I see. Thank you, sir. Our next guest this evening has been called America's greatest woman poet. And yet during her own time there were probably not more than a dozen people who were even aware that she wrote poetry. She produced over eighteen hundred poems but only *three* were published during her lifetime!

She was born in Amherst, Massachusetts, at a time when the life and culture of New England were perhaps at their fullest flower. Even for a long time after her death in 1886, at the age of fifty-six, her genius was still unrecognized. As late as 1921 the combined sales of all volumes of Emily Dickinson's poems amounted to only *214 copies!*

Incredible as it seems, Americans might never have known of the brilliance of Emily Dickinson had they not been told about it by the English. Two Emily Dickinson books published in London in the 1920s suddenly established her international reputation after the long years of neglect. Ladies and gentlemen, Miss Emily Dickinson.

(Emily Dickinson enters, somewhat timidly.) (Superimpose: Emily Dickinson 1830–1886.)

STEVE: Good evening, Miss Dickinson. We are honored to have you here, particularly because for part of your lifetime, we are told, you never appeared in public.

EMILY: That is true, Mr. Allen. I have been described as a recluse, a cryptic, a ghost, an eccentric. In fact, I was painfully shy with strangers. Even at this moment I confess that I am not entirely at ease, but I could not resist the opportunity to share the company of your distinguished guests.

DARWIN: It is our honor, I assure you, dear lady. Any poet who could describe a storm as "inciting a strange mob of panting trees" is well worth meeting.

EMILY: Thank you.

DARWIN: And, just think, we shall also be meeting Galileo.

EMILY: Isn't that wonderful!

STEVE: Do you think, Dr. Darwin, that Galileo is so important purely because of his scientific discoveries?

DARWIN: No, I think not. I would say that one of the fundamentally important things about Galileo is that by means of his discoveries he forced man to become accustomed to reality. Now there may be some comfort in myth and superstition. In fact, I would say definitely that there is such comfort.

For purposes of illustration, let me draw here a deliberately absurd picture: Let us suppose there is a small body of religious worshippers who are convinced that God is a giant cucumber. Let us suppose further that when their loved ones die, members of this faith place cucumber slices all around the coffin, in the belief that to do so is somehow to satisfy and please their deity. Now you and I know that that is an absurd practice, and yet who among us can deny that for those struck by the tragedy of the loss of a loved one the belief is nevertheless reassuring?

But Galileo, as I say, showed that the work of the Creator is far more wonderful, far more astounding, really, than primitive myth had suggested.

STEVE: You showed quite the same thing yourself.

DARWIN: *(Modestly.)* Well, before this man, science in the modern sense of the word hardly existed. A few scattered individuals, in speculating on science, had made a few isolated remarkable discoveries; but in most instances what was valid about their work was mixed up with a great deal of nonsense.

STEVE: Would it be safe to say that the intellectual history of modern science, properly so called, really begins with Signor Galileo Galilei?

DARWIN: Yes, of course! It was he, after all, who changed man's ideas about the concept of "motion." And what is science, I ask you, but the study of matter in motion?

STEVE: Ladies and gentlemen, Signor Galileo Galilei. *(Galileo enters.) (Superimpose: Galileo Galilei 1564–1642.)*

STEVE: Welcome, sir.

GALILEO: It is my pleasure, Mr. Allen.

EMILY: You know, one thing that has always pleased me about the men of the Renaissance is that though they were curious about science, their technical investigations did not preclude an interest in poetry and the other arts.

DARWIN: Quite so, Miss Dickinson. Signor Galileo was fully interested in the arts and in living the "good life." What was it,

Signor, that you once said about wine?

GALILEO: *(He chuckles.)* I said, "Il Vino era luce impasse con humore."

STEVE: Which means—

GALILEO: Wine is light, held together by water.

DARWIN: Yes. You see, it was inevitable that this man would arouse jealousy, even in the absence of his dazzling scientific accomplishments. He spoke and wrote with great brilliance. He was a musician. He was even a painter. And, like myself, he loved to contemplate his garden, his flowers and plants.

EMILY: In which regard, I suppose, he was rather typical of his age. We associate you with the city of Florence, Signor. Was that the place of your birth?

GALILEO: No, Miss Dickinson, I was born in Pisa, in 1564.

EMILY: My goodness, 1564. The year Shakespeare was born!

GALILEO: Yes. And the year Michelangelo died.

STEVE: Ah. Well now, our fourth guest. He's a strange, almost legendary figure from a somewhat puzzling period of history, the fifth century. It was the time when the Roman Empire, which had survived for almost a thousand years, was at last crumbling. Attila the Hun was one of the barbarian leaders who struck terror into the hearts of all the Europeans of his day, as he led hundreds of thousands of his people out of the mysterious East.

Ladies and gentlemen, Attila the Hun. *(Attila enters.) (Superimpose: Attila 406–453.)*

STEVE: Welcome, sir.

ATTILA: Thank you. Miss Dickinson. Gentlemen.

STEVE: You know, Attila, most Americans know practically nothing about the Huns. Because the Germans were called Huns in our First World War, some of us think that the original Huns were a German tribe.

GALILEO: Really!

STEVE: I'm afraid so.

GALILEO: Incredible.

STEVE: Tell us, please, where did the Huns originally come from?

ATTILA: Oh, who knows where any people really come from? Usually when people think they're answering that question all they are doing is explaining where their ancestors were living perhaps one thousand years earlier. But you might just as easily go back to that thousand-year-earlier point and ask the question then, Where did a particular group come from? There were legends among my people that not long after the time of Christ the Chinese drove the Hiung-Mu people westward out of Mongolia. Half of us stopped our migration in Afghanistan, while the other group pushed farther west, into what is now known as Eastern Europe. To this day I understand the Turks consider us their ancestors.

What little I know about the early history of my people leads me to believe they came from what are now the plains of Mongolia. The Mongols, I understand, survive unto the present day.

EMILY: Yes, but they are an Oriental people.

ATTILA: So?

STEVE: You know, that's interesting. People who have visited the Soviet Union report that in the streets of Moscow today you can see some Mongols, and even some Russians of mixed blood, with decidedly Oriental features.

ATTILA: Of course. As a matter of fact, how anybody on the earth today can possibly talk of a pure-blooded human stock is more than I can understand. People who think that they are pure-blooded Germans or pure-blooded Italians or Irish or whatever are simply deluding themselves.

EMILY: Why do you say that?

ATTILA: Because for thousands of years across the face of Europe, and the other continents as well, there has been an endless process of migration, war, pillage, rape, intermarriage, and intermingling of all kinds. My fighting men did not bring their wives along on their campaigns, I assure you. No, it's a rare man who can accurately trace his ancestry back three or four generations with complete certainty.

In any event, my people originally came out of the East and slowly moved westward across the face of Europe.

STEVE: What was your main activity? How did you support yourself?

ATTILA: By war, chiefly. We naturally kept cattle and did a bit of farming. But we were great natural horsemen, and there was something in us that made us want to explore and dominate the areas unknown to us.

EMILY: How dreadful.

STEVE: What were some of the tribes you dominated?

ATTILA: The first people we conquered were the Russians. We

moved into their territories in the year 355, attacked and gradually absorbed a number of their tribes. About twenty years later
we did battle with the Ostrogoths.

STEVE: The Ostrogoths. Where did they live?

ATTILA: In the Ukraine.

EMILY: How did you treat the tribes you conquered?

ATTILA: I understand you have a modern expression, "If you can't
beat 'em, join 'em." Actually that was quite a common process
in my day. When our armies were victorious, the people we
defeated—those that were not killed anyway—usually were
willing to join us, thus enlarging our forces. Gradually we
moved farther west and defeated the Visigoths, in part of what
is now called Germany.

    You know, I almost have to feel sorry for the poor Visigoths.

DARWIN: Why is that?

ATTILA: Well, they not only had *us* to worry about, but they had a
more complicated problem. They turned to their rear and
appealed to the Roman Emperor Valens for permission to cross
the Danube and settle in Roman-controlled territory, just to get
away from *us*. The Romans said it would be all right for them to
come in and then fell on them when they did.

    As a result of the deceit and treachery of the Romans, the
Goths eventually pulled themselves together and started a separate war with them. In 378 the Romans suffered their most
disastrous defeat in almost 600 years. And they deserved it!

GALILEO: What accounted for the defeat of the Roman armies?

ATTILA: Well, my own guess is that the Goths prevailed because
they had learned something from the strategy of us Huns. We
moved across the continent so easily because we were on horseback. And it was the Gothic cavalry, you see, that defeated the
Roman infantry.

GALILEO: Ah, yes, I remember having read of that engagement. As
a matter of fact it was the victory of cavalry over foot soldiers in
that battle that largely dictated military strategy for the next
thousand years.

STEVE: I see. Well, now, at what point in history, Attila, did you
personally appear on the scene?

ATTILA: I'll tell you. Things went from bad to worse for the Romans, and finally in 410 the city of Rome itself fell and was
pillaged by the Goths. Part of the Gothic force that took Rome
consisted of Huns, and the Goths had trouble controlling them.

At more or less that same time another powerful tribe called the Vandals began to make their presence known. They came mostly from the provinces of what is now called East Germany and gradually moved to the south into Hungary.

As the weakness of Rome became increasingly plain, the Vandals took advantage of the situation and ravaged all of Gaul. You now call that general area France. In the year 409 about one hundred thousand Vandals entered Spain. In 433 my uncle King Rua of the Huns died, and control of his armies was thrown to me and my brother Bleda. When Bleda was killed I took over.

STEVE: Some historians suspect, sir, that you were responsible for your brother's death.

ATTILA: *(He glares malevolently.)* You can go to hell.

EMILY: Oh, my goodness.

STEVE: Well, were you as ruthless a conqueror as people today seem to think?

ATTILA: I don't care what people today think, but I was a military man, so I used whatever degree of force was necessary in any given situation. And as I look about the world today I don't see that things have changed terribly much in that regard. *(He laughs, remembering.)*

Come to think of it, I did employ an idea that I think you moderns have developed quite a bit. It's what you call *propaganda*.

STEVE: Propaganda?

ATTILA: Yes. As soon as my forces had come into an area, and were threatening adjacent tribes, I would send some of my men out to tell horrible stories about my cruelty. *(He laughs again.)*

You see, I figured out that if you can strike terror into people's hearts you can save your own troops a lot of trouble. People are more inclined to give up before a fight than to stand against you.

STEVE: The Europeans never saw through this?

ATTILA: Not very often; you must remember that the Europeans were almost totally ignorant, uneducated, illiterate, and superstitious. Since practically everything they believed was myth and nonsense, they were guided largely by their fears. So I was able to take advantage of their cowardly imaginations, to terrify them with, I suppose, less actual bloodshed than I might otherwise have had to employ.

EMILY: Were you yourself able to read and write?

ATTILA: No, lady, I was not. In my day only scholars— churchmen—could read.

EMILY: Why didn't they share their knowledge with the poor peasants?

ATTILA: A good question. But I was no savage; get that straight. I had my own definition of honor, and I thought that it was important to assure men that they would be justly treated if they did what they were told.

STEVE: Did you live by a moral code?

ATTILA: *(He frowns, annoyed.)* As regards my personal morals, sir, they were superior, I assure you, to those of many of the Romans. In my capital, the city now called Budapest, I lived a simple life. I drank very sparingly and had no interest in luxury and riches.

GALILEO: Yes, Miss Dickinson, Attila is quite right when he observes that he was no ignorant, barbarian savage. By the middle of the fifth century he was the most powerful man in Europe, and the two emperors, Theodosius II and Valentinian, both paid him tribute.

DARWIN: But see here, Attila! The murderous raids of your army of half-a-million men caused devastation and ruin across the face of Europe, for centuries! It was over four hundred years before the Balkans recovered from the scourge of your military forces. While you were no ignorant savage in one sense it can hardly be argued that a man who would massacre the inhabitants of hundreds of cities across Russia, Germany, and France was civilized!

ATTILA: I wasn't aware, Darwin, that the *British* Empire was built by *pacifists*!

STEVE: How were you finally defeated?

ATTILA: Well, in 451 Theodoric the First, the old bastard who was king of the Visigoths, made an alliance with the Romans, and their combined armies attacked mine near Troyes. It was one of the bloodiest battles in the history of mankind. My half-a-million men against hundreds of thousands of theirs!

GALILEO: Yes, it was like a scene out of *The Inferno*. A hundred-and-sixty-two-thousand men are said to have been killed in that battle!

EMILY: How horrible!

ATTILA: Oh, are you shocked at the number of deaths. Well,

understand this! The hundred and sixty-two thousand who died at Troyes were military men, who knew of their risks. You're an American, right lady? And *you*, sir? Well, I understand that in Hiroshima and Nagasaki in this century American forces killed just about one-hundred-sixty-thousand mostly civilian men, women, and children in just a few minutes, and the Japanese themselves killed millions!

EMILY: Yes, but modern nations at least try to avoid war, because —

ATTILA: I don't mind your being shocked, or saddened, by the prospect of bloody, painful death. Such reactions are, after all, your privilege to feel. But what I will not tolerate is the suggestion that you people today are somehow more civilized, or more compassionate, than the men of my day. If we were killers, then we were. But at least we were not hypocrites.

STEVE: But, surely, Attila, there's a difference between —

ATTILA: Listen to me! In *your* Second World War do you know how many people were killed?

STEVE: No. How many were?

ATTILA: Forty million! Yes, 40 *million* people were killed, by the supposedly civilized modern nations! Think of that number of deaths, my friends. Roll the figure around in your minds. Forty million killed, a very large percentage of them *civilians*!

Now perhaps a *pacifist*, or a *saint*, might be able to call me to moral account on the basis of his own spiritual superiority. But I'll be damned if I'll take such criticism from the likes of those who rule the world *today*!

STEVE: Well, perhaps we'd better change the subject. Let's put some questions to Dr. Darwin about his theory of evolution.

GALILEO: Good idea. What do you think led you into your field of specialization, Darwin?

DARWIN: Well, Signor Galileo, when I was quite a young child I read a book called *The Natural History of Selborne*, by a clergyman named Gilbert White who can be called, I think, the father of natural field history. This marvelous book got me interested in ornithology, the study of birds. That interest in turn led me to beetle hunting, the collection of minerals, and a fascination with nature generally.

STEVE: Was your father a man of science?

DARWIN: Well, he was a doctor. A remarkable man, my father. He was very successful, quite intelligent; the kind of man some might describe as domineering.

EMILY: He sounds rather like my own.

GALILEO: And mine.

ATTILA: My father, too, was no bargain.

DARWIN: Well, in 1825 he sent me to Edinburgh to study medicine. But I'm afraid the field held no interest for me. I was appalled at witnessing operations and the dissection of human corpses.

GALILEO: It's interesting, Darwin. You and I both turned away from medicine.

DARWIN: Yes, quite. But I had the great good fortune at about that time to hear some lectures by the great American artist Audubon.

STEVE: Yes, we now have what is called the Audubon Society.

DARWIN: Well, Audubon drew those remarkable pictures of birds, you know, and he knew a great deal about this branch of biology.

EMILY: How did your father react to your lack of interest in medicine, Dr. Darwin?

DARWIN: Rather sternly, I'm afraid. He decided—without consulting my own wishes—that if I was not cut out for medicine, then I should enter the ministry.

EMILY: Oh, dear. Did you resist?

DARWIN: No. Since my interest in birds was something I viewed more as a hobby than a profession, I did not resist. In 1828 I entered Christ's College at Cambridge, with the intention of becoming a clergyman.

EMILY: Did you become one?

DARWIN: No, but as a matter of fact, Miss Dickinson, I rather liked the thought of being a country clergyman. It seemed a pleasant, even charming life. It never struck me at the time how illogical it was to say that I believed what I could not understand—and what is, in fact, partly unintelligible.

EMILY: But isn't that where faith comes in?

DARWIN: *(He smiles.)* Perhaps I had no gift for theology. I believe there are gifts for such things, just as there are gifts disposing us to aptitudes in the sciences or arts. Anyway, after I had completed my education I received a marvelous invitation from a gentleman named George Peacock, an invitation that changed my life forever.

STEVE: Who was George Peacock?

DARWIN: He was a renowned mathematician and astronomer at Cambridge University, and it was up to him to decide what naturalists might be nominated to travel on the surveying ships of the Royal Navy. At that time the *Beagle*, a 242-ton brig, was scheduled to make a trip around the world. Professor Peacock wondered if I wanted to sign on. The idea, of course, intrigued me.

STEVE: What was your father's reaction?

DARWIN: Unfortunately he was bitterly against it. He said to me, "If you can find any man of common sense who advises you to go, I will give my consent."

Fortunately at that point my uncle Josiah Wedgwood II intervened to tell my father that the proposed trip was a marvelous idea!

STEVE: Wedgwood, you say?

DARWIN: Yes, of the family famous for its china dishware.

EMILY: How old were you when you made the trip?

DARWIN: I was only twenty-two. We set sail from Plymouth on December 27, 1831.

STEVE: On a long or short voyage?

DARWIN: Oh, it was five long years before I returned to England.

It seems to me now that those five years constituted my real education. When I returned home my notebook was crammed full of facts, my head was swimming with ideas, and I had countless boxes full of specimens I'd accumulated here and there around the world.

GALILEO: And from your studies of nature you began to develop certain theories?

DARWIN: Precisely! One of the most remarkable ideas that had gradually formed in my mind on that trip grew out of my observation of *rocks*.

STEVE: Rocks?

DARWIN: *(He shows a fossil in rock.)* Yes! You see, I found many fossil skeletons of mammals and other creatures in these rocks, at various heights and depths, in mountain ranges, and elsewhere.

STEVE: And what did that suggest to you?

GALILEO: Before Dr. Darwin responds, pause and consider the situation! Put yourself in his place. You are looking at a piece of stone that is perhaps a million years old. In it you find the fossil trace of an insect or a mole. Ask yourself, What does this mean? This is science in action!

DARWIN: Quite. Well, the fossils of course showed that animal life was perhaps as old as the rock formations themselves, which is to say *millions* of years old. That may not seem like a very remarkable assertion today, but a century ago it was absolutely revolutionary! Simple people, you see, believed the earth itself was only a few *thousand* years old.

EMILY: I was one of those simple people, Dr. Darwin.

DARWIN: Forgive me, Miss Dickinson. No offense intended.

    Another thing that had impressed me during the five-year voyage was the great variation, the differences, I encountered among animals of a particular species. I would see a certain fox or a bird or a cat in one place and then discover that hundreds of miles away that same species was considerably *modified*. The head might be a different shape or the legs longer or something of the sort.

GALILEO: A thrilling discovery! How I envy you!

DARWIN: Well, it became clear to me, from this sort of evidence, that species of animals do not remain constant over the long span of time but gradually change—*evolve*.

ATTILA: I don't believe that!

DARWIN: Well, it's so, Attila, I assure you. You see, one reason a particular animal will exist in one form on one continent and in another form somewhere else must be because different physical circumstances in the two places brought different forces to bear on the species.

EMILY: Fascinating!

DARWIN: Thank you. Evidence supporting this hypothesis was particularly clear on the various isolated islands, such as the Galapagos, which are in the area of the equator, about six hundred miles west of Ecuador.

EMILY: Well now, Dr. Darwin, we know that your theories got you into the most dreadful trouble. You were violently criticized, as Signor Galileo was in his day. But what I don't understand is how such commonsense reasoning could have gotten you into such incredible difficulty.

DARWIN: *(He laughs.)* But, my dear woman, the real trouble did not come about until after I had presented to the world the idea that the common ancestry of all living things includes *man*.

GALILEO: *(He laughs.)* Ah! How they must have howled for your blood when you said that!

DARWIN: You're quite right. Perhaps if I had just continued to talk about finches and tortoises and lizards and such creatures, theologians would have taken little notice of my studies. But as it gradually became clear to me that man himself had been just as much a part of the physical evolution as all the other animals, well . . . it was then, as I say, that I was bitterly attacked.

GALILEO: You see, Miss Dickinson, despite what they think, most men are not really looking for truth. They are looking for information that harmonizes with what they already believe.

But wasn't the factor of "natural selection" important to your theories, Dr. Darwin?

DARWIN: Quite so, sir. It was already evident, you see—as I assume it must have been even in your own time—that breeders of plants or animals could actually change the physical appearance of a species. Men might breed dogs for viciousness or horses for strength or another breed of horses for speed, etc. But this was a case of man *controlling* the breeding of such creatures. For a long time I could not understand how such selection could operate in the state of nature in the *absence* of human intervention.

And then, in October of 1838, I happened casually to pick up Malthus's book, *Population*. It was while reading Malthus that the idea of natural selection became clear to me. Here then, at last, I had found a theory by which to work.

GALILEO: Did you publish your ideas at once?

DARWIN: No, I'm afraid not. In fact I kept delaying publication as long as possible. Somehow it seemed important to me to pile up great accumulations of facts in support of my ideas. I would occasionally get close to publication, and then something would frighten me off; and I would assume that I had to advance more arguments, and present more facts, to support my thesis.

It was not until 1842—five years after I had ended the voyage on the *Beagle*—that I allowed myself the satisfaction of writing a simple thirty-five-page abstract of my theory of evolution. I did not publish it in that form, however. Two years later I produced a 230-page version of my argument. But again it seemed that that was not the right time to formally publish my findings. Finally, in the summer of 1858, something happened which prodded me to action. I received a paper from my friend and fellow naturalist Alfred Russell Wallace, who, writing from the Malay archipelago, sent me an essay he had written titled "On the Tendency for Varieties to Depart Indefinitely from the Original Type."

STEVE: I wonder now if Wallace was entitled to assume that there actually were any "original types."

GALILEO: Fascinating question.

ATTILA: I don't understand it.

EMILY: Naturally.

DARWIN: *(He laughs.)* Well, anyway . . . I perceived at once that independently Wallace had arrived at substantially the same point of view that I had developed. Since that time I've always been happy to acknowledge the originality of Wallace's work in this field.

EMILY: Well, when, specifically, did the world finally learn of your views?

DARWIN: I was greatly encouraged, Miss Dickinson, by some of my intimate friends in the field of science, most notably the prominent geologist Charles Lyell and the botanist Joseph Hooker. They kept encouraging me and finally, in July of 1858, my views, and those of Alfred Wallace, were communicated to the Linnean Society and to the world in an edition of that society's journal.

The following year I published *The Origin of Species*, which I had finished in just over thirteen months. Even as it went to press I still viewed it as only an abstract of my views, since I had a great deal more to say about the subject. Only 1,250 copies were printed, and all sold the same day.

GALILEO: What was the initial reaction?

DARWIN: As they say today, sir, there was good news and bad news. One of my former teachers, Adam Sedgwick, said that he found parts of the book utterly false and grievously mischievous!

A leading scientific philosopher of the day, Sir John Herschel, called my theory "the law of higgledy-piggledy."

STEVE: But, happily, a great many wiser heads were convinced that you were on the right track.

DARWIN: Yes, a brilliant young biologist Thomas Henry Huxley immediately became one of my strongest defenders.

STEVE: Well, thank you, Dr. Darwin. That was fascinating.

Now, Miss Dickinson, if we may turn to you, many literary critics have suggested that your life presented a difficult puzzle. Even some of your warmest admirers feel that they've had great difficulty in getting to know the real you.

EMILY: So I understand. I think, to know anyone you should learn something about the social circumstances in which he lives. Dr. Darwin found that different environments produce different animals. Well, they produce different people, too. Life in a simple New England village a century ago was very different from the culture and pace of your large cities today.

STEVE: How so?

EMILY: We enjoyed peace and composure. There were important and dramatic events happening in the outside world at the time, of course. Europe was in turmoil. China was seething. But somehow the noise of such alarms rarely seemed to penetrate the quiet and seclusion of the lovely communities of the New England states.

STEVE: As you look at this photograph of your grave, in the old cemetery of Amherst, what thoughts occur to you?

EMILY: Mmmm. How very New England. That headstone was erected by my niece Martha Dickinson Bianchi, a dear girl.

Ahh, my room is there at the right side, on the second story.

The trees! They're so much taller, so much grander than I remember them. We were surrounded by nature in that time and place, Mr. Allen. Your life today seems to be filled with automobiles and television and things that whir and click and buzz and shock and break and distract. But what I saw from *my* window was the calm, delightful debris of an invisible, honey-slow windstorm that tossed together jasmine and fern, honey-suckle and honeybee, and cherries ripening in the trees, plum and pear trees, blossoms brilliant in the spring, all enveloped in the unforgettable New England greenery.

STEVE: I recall your description of the *sun* of late afternoon as seen from that view.

EMILY: Yes.

> Blazing in Gold and quenching in Purple
> Leaping like Leopards to the Sky
> Then at the feet of the old Horizon
> Laying her spotted Face to die
> Stooping as low as the Otter's Window
> Touching the Roof and tinting the Barn
> Kissing her Bonnet to the Meadow
> And the Juggler of Day is gone.

STEVE: You seem to have had a passionate love affair with nature. What was, or is, nature to you?

EMILY: "Nature" is what we see—

> The Hill—the Afternoon—
> Squirrels—Eclipse—the Bumblebee—
> Nay—Nature is Heaven—

Nature is what we hear—
The Bobolink—The Sea—
Thunder—The Cricket—
Nay—Nature is Harmony—

Nature is what we know—
But have no Art to say—
So impotent Our Wisdom is
To her Simplicity.

DARWIN: Miss Dickinson, it strikes me as very strange that your
poems weren't published during your lifetime. Why was that?

EMILY: I didn't write them for publication, Dr. Darwin. I wrote
them to express my moods, my emotions, and to amuse those I
loved. My sister Lavinia did send a few of my verses to Samuel
Bowles, a friend of our family who was editor of the *Springfield
Massachusetts Republican*, but they were published without my
consent.

STEVE: Do you remember which poems were involved?

EMILY: One was a simple poem about a garter snake.

GALILEO: Ah, yes. I have been leafing through this collection of
your poems, Miss Dickinson, and I must say, I believe this
poem is unsurpassed in the English language.

EMILY: Thank you, Dr. Galileo.

GALILEO: Pray, do recite it for us.

EMILY: A narrow Fellow in the Grass
          Occasionally rides—
          You may have met Him—did you not
          His notice sudden is—

          The Grass divides as with a Comb—
          A spotted shaft is seen—
          And then it closes at your feet
          And opens further on—

          He likes a Boggy Acre
          A Floor too cool for Corn—
          Yet when a Child, and Barefoot—
          I more than once at Morn

          Have passed, I thought, a Whip lash
          Unbraiding in the Sun

When stooping to secure it
It wrinkled, and was gone—

Several of Nature's People
I know, and they know me—
I feel for them a transport
Of cordiality—

But never met this Fellow
Attended, or alone
Without a tighter breathing
And Zero at the Bone—

STEVE: Remarkable! One of my favorite poems is the one you
wrote about butterflies *swimming*, not flying, but swimming in
the air "off banks of noon," I believe is the phrase.

EMILY: Oh, yes.
A Bird came down the Walk—
He did not know I saw—
He bit an Angleworm in halves
And *ate* the fellow, raw.

And then he drank a Dew
From a convenient Grass—
And then hopped sideways to the Wall
To let a Beetle pass—

He glanced with rapid eyes
Then hurried all around—
They looked like frightened Beads, I thought—
He stirred his Velvet Head

Like one in danger, Cautious,
I offered him a Crumb
And he unrolled his feathers
And rowed him softer home—

Than Oars divide the Ocean,
Too silver for a seam—
Or Butterflies, off Banks of Noon
Leap, plashless, as they swim.

GALILEO: Beautiful!

EMILY: Thank you, sir.

STEVE: Miss Dickinson, you've described yourself as shy. But those who knew you as a young girl report quite the opposite.

EMILY: *(Nervously.)* I do not wish to discuss my . . . personal life.

STEVE: But people are curious to know how you changed from a cheerful young—

EMILY: *(Curtly.)* Yes, people are very curious, aren't they? But why must their curiosity be satisfied?

GALILEO: Well, was yours a happy childhood, Miss Dickinson?

EMILY: For the most part, yes. I often knew the most intense happiness. I tried to express as much once, in these lines:

> If all the griefs I am to have
> Would only come today,
> I am so happy, I believe
> They'd laugh and run away.
>
> If all the joys I am to have
> Would only come today,
> They could not be so big as this
> That happens to me now.

STEVE: Well, now, there obviously was, in your life, a sharp transition. A happy, carefree New England childhood. But your later life is a—

EMILY: My later life is my own business.

DARWIN: But it's a pity, Miss Dickinson, that perhaps because we know too little about you, you remain an enigmatic figure!

EMILY: If I do, Dr. Darwin, it is not really because you have accumulated so few facts about me. What little we know, about anything, might be likened to a grain of sand compared to the boundless Sahara of what-might-be-known. But, don't you see, this is true of individual human beings, too! I tried to express the idea once, in this poem to a dear companion.

> But Susan is a stranger yet;
> The ones who like her most
> Have never scaled her haunted house
> Nor compromised her ghost.
>
> To pity those who know her not
> Is helped by the regret

> That those who know her, know her less
> The nearer her they get.

So you see, even when we are very close to another the horizon of his soul endlessly recedes from us.

Even if we try to look within ourselves, the same is true. The Greek admonition "Know thyself" points to an ideal. An ideal is endlessly striven for, but can never be achieved.

If you will permit me the temerity of a critical judgment, gentlemen, I am utterly unable to comprehend the modern insistence on the right of the public to pry into everything, on publicity, on brazen public display. The right to privacy seems almost to have vanished in this century. I lived with the uncompromising conviction that my personal life was somehow sacred and of no legitimate concern to the public. I felt that I had the right to live and die in obscurity, though I was aware that my view was solitary. I expressed the observation in these lines:

> The right to perish might be thought
> An undisputed right—
> *Attempt* it, and the Universe
> Upon the *opposite*
> Will concentrate its officers—
> You cannot even die
> But nature and mankind must pause
> To pay you scrutiny.

Now, please, gentlemen, that will be quite enough questions about me. Let us hear from Dr. Galileo!

STEVE: Very well. I hold further questions, for a while. But I reserve the right to put a few more to you, if I may.

In case you've just joined us, we're visiting with four distinguished personages from history. In this order: Charles Darwin, poet Emily Dickinson, Attila the Hun, and Galileo Galilei. I confess that every time I say your name, sir, I feel as if I'm yodeling. *Galileo Galilei.*

Well now, you told us earlier your people were Florentines.

GALILEO: Yes: They gave me a happy, secure childhood, and at seventeen I entered the University of Pisa to study philosophy and medicine.

DARWIN: Ah, how I wish I could travel back in time, Galileo, to those great universities of Pisa, of Bologna, of Paris.

GALILEO: Yes, Signor, they were exciting. But I must say that I was displeased by their dogmatic Scholasticism, in which Aristotle was the beginning and end of all argument.

ATTILA: You were opposed to the Greek philosopher?

GALILEO: Oh not fully, though he did make errors. But I began to get the impression that Aristotle was not used—as he should have been—to encourage one's own reason, but he was used as a cover for dogmatic repetition.

DARWIN: It's by no means a simple question as to what extent we should respect intellectual authority.

GALILEO: You're quite right. Naturally we must pay the most careful attention to what the great minds of earlier ages have discovered. They have much wisdom to teach us. But we must never let our admiration for these great men blind us to the fact that they were only human. For their humanity means that they will inevitably fall into error at certain times.

Now in my day all learned people had enormous respect for Aristotle. He was a great philosopher. But as a scientist, as you might say, not so hot. Aristotle taught that the heavens, which is to say the stars and planets, are *perfect*, in comparison to the earth, which is *imperfect*.

STEVE: That's ridiculous.

GALILEO: *(He smiles.)* Where were you when I needed you?

Anyway, if Aristotle were right it seemed logically to follow that the earth could not be a moving planet like those in the heavens. And since the only alternative to *movement* is *rest*, even scholars in my day therefore assumed that the earth was *motionless*. For a long time, you see, rigid belief in the teachings of Aristotle simply blinded men to the physical realities about them.

STEVE: Well, you'd think that simple common sense would—

GALILEO: Ah, no, sir. Beware of common sense. Our senses, you see, can both inform us and lead us astray. Demonstration. Attila, my friend—

ATTILA: Yes?

GALILEO: Would you say that the *sun* and the *moon* are approximately the same size?

ATTILA: Yes, of course they are.

GALILEO: Precisely. Because to the naked eye they appear so. But your sense of sight misleads you. The moon is actually much smaller than the earth, while the sun is many times larger than the earth.

To determine such questions we should employ the methods of science! Now my telescope showed that as regards the question of the movement of the earth Aristotle was as wrong as could be.

Anyway, by 1588 I was lecturing in Pisa and, I'm afraid, already, at that early point, making enemies.

STEVE: How did that come about?

GALILEO: Well, Don Giovanni de'Medici, who was governor of the Port of Leghorn, planned to use a certain hydraulic machine to empty the wet dock there. When I examined the machine, I saw its faults and predicted that it would fail. It did and, of course, there are few things as dangerous for a critic as being correct.

The Medici, you understand, were totalitarians at heart. It was always dangerous to oppose them openly.

I thought it would be better for my health, as they say, to accept a post at the University of Padua, which placed me under the jurisdiction of the beautiful republic of Venice.

STEVE: Did your fortunes fare better in the Venetian republic?

GALILEO: Yes. There I did important work on mechanics, on *spherical geometry*, and on fortifications.

ATTILA: Fortifications? So you, too, were a military man.

GALILEO: In a sense, yes.

EMILY: So you prospered in Venice?

GALILEO: Well, yes and no. There was one problem. You see, it was impossible to obtain from such a republic—however splendid and generous—a salary without duties attached to it.

My problem was that I preferred to lecture, to write, and to study. Unfortunately the calls upon my services by the republic did not permit me enough time for these endeavors. I required, you see, a certain amount of ease and leisure, but it was difficult to arrange such a schedule at that time. I eventually concluded, therefore, that I should, after all, work in the service of an absolute prince.

STEVE: To get back to the matter of the telescope, sir, the Polish monk Copernicus had advanced the theory that the sun was the center of the planetary system, almost a hundred years before you did similar work. Was expressing your views then really so dangerous to you?

GALILEO: Oh, very much so. As I wrote to Kepler in 1597, long after I had accepted the heliocentric theory I did not wish to talk about it publicly because I was fearful of meeting the same fate as our dear master Copernicus, who although he earned himself immortal fame amongst a few, yet amongst a far greater number was only worthy of hooting and derision, so great is the number of fools.

But by the year 1610 I could no longer keep silent because I had learned so much through my studies of the heavens with the telescope. In that year I published my *Message from the Stars*, announcing both the invention of the telescope and my support of the theories of Copernicus.

ATTILA: What was the response?

GALILEO: Opposition! The academic people from the universities of Pisa, Padua, Bologna, and elsewhere were almost totally hostile. They seemed to place more store on what our old friend Aristotle had said many centuries earlier than on the scientific evidence available to their own senses. And, of course, many of them referred to the infallibility of the Scriptures.

EMILY: Was the Church totally opposed to you?

GALILEO: Oh, no. Many of my friends and supporters were themselves churchmen. For example, the brilliant monk Benedetto Castelli, who was the professor of mathematics at Pisa. And the famous Jesuit astronomer Father Clavius, who really did the work on *calendar reform* for which Pope Gregory has been given credit. Father Clavius, though he at first laughed at my discoveries, was wise enough to look through my telescope. Once he did so, he conceded that my reports were in substance correct.

EMILY: Then you got along well with many churchmen?

GALILEO: But of course. On an earlier program of this series one of your guests was Thomas Aquinas; and I understand that he explained to you that his order, the Dominicans, were specialists in detecting, and combating, heresy.

STEVE: Yes, that's correct.

GALILEO: Then you will understand why most of my troubles were with the Dominicans, the policemen of philosophy.

DARWIN: Were your arguments, in fact, sir, opposed to the Scriptures?

GALILEO: Not at all, Dr. Darwin. I said at the time: Though Scripture cannot be mistaken, the *interpreters* of it are liable to error in many ways. And one mistake in particular would be most serious: If we always stop short at the literal significance of the words of the Bible. For in this way not only many contradictions would be apparent, but even grave heresies and blasphemies. For then it would be necessary to give God hands and feet and ears and human and bodily emotions—such as anger, repentance, hatred—and sometimes forgetfulness of things past, as well as ignorance of the future.

In Scripture, you see, there are found many propositions which, taking the bare literal sense of the word, must be contrary to the truth. But they are placed there in such phraseology in order to accommodate themselves to the capacity of the uneducated. Consequently, for those who merit to be separated from the crowd, it is necessary for them to produce the true meaning of Scripture and to explain to the uneducated the particular reasons why certain wordings have been presented.

Now there may be doubts and arguments as to passages of Scripture, problems of translation, etc. But there should be no room for doubt or argument about the evident facts of the physical world about us. Nature—unlike the sometimes confusingly worded Scriptures—is inexorable and immutable and does not care one jot whether her secret reasons and modes of operation be above or below the capacity of man's understanding!

This is the reason then—to accommodate itself to the mental capacities of simple men of the countryside—that Scripture sometimes veils in shadow its principal dogmas.

EMILY: I still find it hard, Signor Galileo, to understand how such reasonable arguments could have stirred up such opposition.

GALILEO: *(He chuckles.)* It seems to me, dear lady, that clear, unvarnished statements of the truth can place a man in danger even in the present day if what he says displeases either the ruling powers or the uninformed sentiments of the masses.

STEVE: Just who was it that attacked you?

GALILEO: Oh, many. Among them, for example, the Bishop of Fiesole, who wished to have not only me punished but also suggested that Copernicus should be imprisoned! He was surprised to be told that Copernicus had been *dead* for many years.

STEVE: And you said the Dominicans got after you.

GALILEO: Yes. I did, however, receive a beautiful letter of apology from Father Maraffi, the preacher-general of the Dominicans, who said, "Unfortunately I have to answer for all the idiocies that thirty or forty thousand of my brothers may and actually do commit."

ATTILA: Thirty or forty thousand people can commit a lot of idiocies.

GALILEO: *(He laughs.)* Yes, indeed. In 1615 Father Lurinie, and other Dominicans, brought some of my writings to the attention of the Inquisition.

STEVE: Ah, the Inquisition. Almost all historical references to the Inquisition are highly critical of it, but I—

EMILY: Are you implying there could be any justification for it?!

GALILEO: I believe there was.

STEVE: Really?

GALILEO: Let me explain. To understand the Inquisition one must understand the European period of history from which it emerged.

The Protestant Reformation had taken place, followed by the Catholic Counter-Reformation. But, sad to say, Europe was approaching the disastrous Thirty Years' War, a war of religion.

ATTILA: Christians slaughtering other Christians.

GALILEO: Alas, yes. It was a very unstable time. Consequently rulers, and many of the people too—both Catholic and Protestant—thought that unanimity of opinion about religious matters was a necessary condition for personal and state security.

Even today—and you Americans consider yours a *free country*—there is a great middle-of-the-road consensus, a strong conservative bias against people who have what may seem eccentric or unusual views.

DARWIN: That is true. Even in modern times if a pacifist or a vegetarian or a socialist or a person with any unusual theory speaks out publicly, even though he may not always be arrested and imprisoned, nevertheless he is sometimes literally in physical danger. So do not think that the present period is that much better than the past in that regard!

GALILEO: Now some of the problems in my day grew out of a point of view expressed by Thomas Aquinas when he said that since it was obvious that the *soul* was more important than the body; therefore it logically followed that if imprisonment and execution were suitable punishment for those who harmed only the body, they were also suitable punishments for those who harmed the *soul*. By which he meant those who preached doctrines contrary to dominant religious belief.

EMILY: *(Haughtily.)* Well, I must say, that in the New England of my day Protestant leaders, at least, were not so cruel and dogmatic.

GALILEO: Dear lady, you led a very sheltered life. Neither Protestants nor Catholics can be particularly proud of the record of the way in which they have dealt with those who dared to speak out against them.

DARWIN: Yes, sad to say, Christians of all kinds have thought it quite permissible to use the most hideous torture: to throw people into monstrous prison dungeons without proper trial, to hang them, to burn them alive, in order, as it was thought, to save their souls and to save the State.

GALILEO: Precisely. It was the great Protestant leader Calvin, do not forget, who approved the burning of the Unitarian Servetus, in Geneva in 1553. And it was the very honored Cardinal Bellarmine, who was ultimately canonized by Pope Pius XI, who drew up the declaration of the Inquisition which brought the great philosopher Giordano Bruno to be *burned at* the stake in the year 1600!

EMILY: But in New England we—

DARWIN: Miss Dickinson, I understand that the Protestants of New England were persecuting and killing witches shortly thereafter.

GALILEO: But I say this about Bellarmine, even though I was condemned, the great Jesuit was my friend and supporter. *(He laughs.)*

STEVE: What's so funny?

GALILEO: I've just remembered. Bellarmine's own book on politics, titled *Controversies*, was put on the index of forbidden books in 1590 because some of his arguments displeased the Pope. *(He laughs.)* Anyway on March 3 in the year 1616, Cardinal Bellarmine announced that I submitted. I thereafter observed eight years of almost total silence on matters which were of the greatest importance to me.

EMILY: What was your family life like during this time, Signor Galileo?

GALILEO: The question is moderately embarrassing, Miss Dickinson, in that, though I had three children by my beloved Marina Gambi, we were never married. I placed my two daughters, in 1611, in a convent. The oldest, Polissena, who was then 13, became a nun.

STEVE: One-hundred-twenty letters from your daughter, Signor, running from 1623 to her death in 1634, have been preserved.

GALILEO: Ah. Well, anyone reading them will know of the great love that this beautiful creature and I felt for each other. Perhaps I cannot have been so bad a person, Miss Dickinson, to have been blessed with such a fine daughter, eh?

DARWIN: You eventually broke the silence imposed on you by the Church, didn't you?

GALILEO: Yes. I felt free to do so because my friend Cardinal Maffeo Barbarini had been elected pope in 1623, taking the name Urban VIII. I continued to write and to speak, but eventually, in 1633, I was convicted by the Holy Office in Rome and strongly condemned.

EMILY: What about your friend, the Pope?

GALILEO: Sad to say, Urban was not a good ruler of the Church. He became far more interested in advancing the temporal, military, and financial power of the papacy than in matters of spiritual leadership.

ATTILA: What's wrong with that?

GALILEO: Well, one hardly expects it in the Vicar of Christ.

Anyway he was a warlike man. During the Thirty Years' War Pope Urban was willing to make a secret alliance with the Protestant ruler of the North, Gustavus Adolphus.

Urban was outmaneuvered in the long run by his rival, Cardinal Richelieu. And in the end he opposed me. I must say, however, that the Pope made certain that during my trial I should not be confined to a cell but assigned to comfortable lodgings, and given a personal servant.

DARWIN: This is far better treatment, I am sure, than the totalitarians of the *present* century have accorded their heretics.

GALILEO: Yes. On June 16, 1636, the Holy Congregation decreed that I was to be *interrogated* as regards my intentions, even, if necessary, by physical *torture* —

EMILY: No!

GALILEO: Yes. That I must *reject* my public views, that I was to be *condemned* to imprisonment at the pleasure of the Holy Congregation, and that I was forbidden to ever again announce my former teachings.

STEVE: Some of your critics, sir, have argued that you did not stand up to the Inquisition in as forceful a manner as you might have.

ATTILA: All I can wish for Galileo's critics is that they suffer his misfortunes.

GALILEO: *(He smiles.)* Thank you. There is no doubt that I might have acted more heroically. But I say, by way of explanation, that I was then an old man, not in the best of health, and mindful that others had actually been burned, tortured, and imprisoned when they had incurred the wrath of the Church. Permit me. *(He strikes two large kitchen matches together.)*

My friend, could you hold your finger in this flame for just a few moments?

STEVE: Of course not.

GALILEO: Yes. The pain, even on just the tip of your finger, would be excruciating. Now perhaps this dry and musty phrase "burned at the stake" has more vivid meaning for you!

But all right, I was no hero. I never claimed that I was. In the end I was sent to prison at the pleasure of my judges, and ordered to repeat the Seven Penitential Psalms once a week for three years.

DARWIN: So your books were then placed on the index of forbidden reading matter?

GALILEO: Yes, where they remained for almost two centuries until 1822, at which time Settele, the official Vatican astronomer, was finally able to convince the Church of the folly of its position.

Better late than never, but two hundred years is quite a long time to wait for vindication. *(He suddenly laughs heartily.)*

STEVE: What are you laughing at now?

GALILEO: It has just come back to me that since the encyclical *Providentissimus* of Pope Leo XIII in 1893, my views concerning the interpretations of Scripture have become part of the official doctrine of the Catholic Church!

EMILY: That must give you enormous satisfaction.

GALILEO: All I can hope now, at this moment of history, is that modern man will be more tolerant and understanding of both me and my churchly opponents. As your great modern dissenter Norman Thomas has written, no longer can the men of today's generation boast of the progress you once took for granted. No Inquisition, which after all was concerned for man's eternal salvation, was more cruel than that of Joseph Stalin, concerned for the triumph of his and Communism's earthly power.

STEVE: Karl Marx may return to this series as a guest. If so, I will take up that point with him.

DARWIN: What do you say, Signor Galileo, to the criticism that because of your literary gifts for ridicule, you exasperated your opponents and consequently did much to bring upon yourself the troubles for which you are remembered?

GALILEO: Yes, it has been said that I was a fierce controversialist. But were not the early Christian saints fierce controversialists who in this way made inevitable their destruction by wild animals, crucifixion, or the fires of the stake? It is no respectable argument, sir, to attempt to justify my oppressors by saying that *I* was a gadfly. Of course I was! I had discovered a small fragment of truth, and I felt an obligation to preach it abroad. As I have said, I was very far from being a hero. And I never considered myself a *martyr*. But this does not make those who persecuted me any the more noble.

STEVE: Well, Miss Dickinson, gentlemen, unfortunately we've run out of time. But will you all join us soon again for a continuation of this most interesting discussion?

ALL: *(They murmur their assent.)*

STEVE: Very well.

When we gather again, Signor Galilei will tell us more of the scientific views that got him into such trouble.

Dr. Darwin will, I trust, tell us more of his remarkable theories.

Attila will give us some of his comments on the world today and tell of his battles with the Romans.

And Miss Dickinson, I very much hope, will recite for us more of her engaging poetry.

SHOW #6

Charles Darwin
(MURRAY MATHESON)

Emily Dickinson
(KATHERINE HELMOND)

Galileo Galilei
(ALEXANDER SCOURBY)

Attila the Hun
(KHIGH DHIEGH)

&
Steve Allen

Welcome to "Meeting of Minds," the program that brings
you great figures from history tonight starring:

From nineteenth-century England—Charles Darwin.

From sixteenth-century Italy—Galileo Galilei.

From nineteenth-century America—poet Emily Dickinson.

From fifth-century Europe—Attila the Hun.

And now your host, Steve Allen.

STEVE: Thank you. Welcome again to "Meeting of Minds." We
bring back first the remarkable gentleman who shook the world
with his theory of evolution. Once again, Dr. Charles Darwin.
(Darwin enters.) (Superimpose: Charles Darwin, 1809–1882.)

STEVE: Good evening, Dr. Darwin. It's good to have you back with
us.

DARWIN: My pleasure, sir.

STEVE: Last week we discussed the difficulties you encountered
when many clergymen assumed that you intended your
theories in part as an attack upon revealed religion.

DARWIN: Yes, it was all utterly absurd. I do think it is far more
complimentary to God to suggest that He set in order the really
wonderfully complex process of evolution than to suggest that,
to use a modern expression, He simply went "zap" in a number
of directions and *magically* created the birds, fishes, and so
forth.

And I am extremely gratified, Mr. Allen, to observe that
today all the leading Christian scholars in the world have no
trouble at all in accepting my theories, while still holding to
their faith in the Bible.

STEVE: We bring back next that puzzling figure, the barbarian
ruler whose forces struck terror into millions of hearts in fifth-
century Europe, Attila the Hun. *(Attila enters.) (Superimpose:
Attila the Hun, 406–453.)*

ATTILA: Gentlemen.

STEVE: Welcome back, sir.

During your last visit, Attila, you were telling us that in the
year 451 your armies swept down into the Italian Peninsula and
eventually stood before the gates of Rome itself. But then you
halted.

DARWIN: Yes, why did you not proceed to take the city?

ATTILA: For several reasons. One was that my armies were troubled by sickness and infection. Also at that time I hoped to
marry the daughter of the Eastern Emperor. And lastly I was

impressed by the arguments of Pope Leo I, who personally led an embassy out to meet me.

STEVE: I see. What sort of man was Leo?

DARWIN: He was one of the truly great popes, Mr. Allen. Some scholars feel that he was actually the first bishop of Rome who could correctly be called pope, in the modern sense of the word.

ATTILA: Well, there was something about Leo that I liked, and respected. Most of the other churchmen I met in that day seemed to me conniving scoundrels. But Leo was an honest man.

Anyway my armies were exhausted, and so was I. I permitted myself to be persuaded by the Pope's arguments.

STEVE: So Rome then was saved?

ATTILA: *(He laughs.)* Not for long. Leo tried the same arguments about a year later with Genseric, the king of the Vandals. But Genseric wouldn't listen to him. His troops attacked Rome from the sea and sacked the city, murdering all who stood in their way.

STEVE: Well, gentlemen, I'd like to bring back now that delicate, strange, brilliant soul from New England, who lived and died in relative obscurity but is now recognized as a truly gifted poet. Miss Emily Dickinson. *(Emily enters.) (Superimpose: Emily Dickinson 1830–1886.)*

STEVE: Good evening, Miss Dickinson.

EMILY: Good evening, gentlemen.

STEVE: You seem . . . er . . . nervous. Is anything wrong?

EMILY: No. But I was so stimulated by meeting these brilliant gentlemen last week that I . . . well, I've been out with lanterns, looking for myself.

STEVE: May I put a few more questions to you?

EMILY: Yes, if you do not pry.

STEVE: Very well. Can you tell us what your education was?

EMILY: I went to school but . . . had no education. When a little girl, I had a friend who taught me immortality . . . but . . . venturing too near it himself . . . he never returned. Soon thereafter my tutor died, and for several years my lexicon was my only companion. Then I found one more, but he was not contented that I be his scholar, so I left the land.

DARWIN: Tell me, Miss Dickinson, who were your early companions?

EMILY: Companions? Oh, hills, sir, and the sundown, and a dog, large as myself, that my father bought me. Dogs are better than human beings in that they know, but do not tell.

STEVE: What can you tell us of your physical surroundings?

EMILY: *(She thinks for a moment.)* The noise in our garden pool at noon excelled the piano!

DARWIN: Your poems about love are justifiably famous. What did love mean to you, Miss Dickinson?

EMILY: *(After a thoughtful moment.)* It is the object of all desire.

> To wait an Hour—is long—
> If Love be just beyond—
> To wait Eternity—is short—
> If love Be at the end—
>
>
> Love is like Life—merely longer
> Love is like Death, daring the Grave
> Love is the Fellow of the Resurrection
> Scooping up the Dust and chanting "Live!"

STEVE: Your poems about love are noted for their . . . uh . . . intensity. Was your home in Amherst, Massachusetts, a loving home? What sort of man was your father?

EMILY: In many respects, a typical product of New England. His nature was formal and his exterior manner cool, though his heart was warm. He loathed public displays of emotion and probably seemed abrupt to those who did not know him well.

STEVE: Was he a well-known man?

EMILY: He served two terms in Congress. My younger sister Lavinia and I loved visiting that awe-inspiring city, Washington.

We lived there, with my father, during the winter of 1853-1854.

STEVE: Ah, yes, 1854. In reading about you the other day I learned that in that year you suffered a great disappointment.

EMILY: *(Nervously.)* Did you, indeed? Well, you're about to suffer one yourself if you think I'm going to discuss such things publicly. Or, for that matter, privately! Can you not be content, sir, with a knowledge of my work?!

STEVE: Well, I really didn't—

EMILY: That a poet suffers . . . should that come as a surprise?

Here! *(She brandishes a piece of manuscript.)* This is what is important!

It's all I have to bring today—
This, and my heart beside—
This, and my heart, and all the fields—
And all the meadows wide—
Be sure you count—should I forget
Some one the sun could tell—
This, and my heart, and all the Bees
Which in the Clover dwell.

DARWIN: Miss Dickinson, your poems are beautiful, and touching.
I'm sure Mr. Allen had no wish to embarrass you. Nor have I.
But, you see, you now belong to the ages. And so when you
write a poem such as "Wild Nights" . . . er . . . would you read
it for us?

EMILY: *(Trapped.)* No!

STEVE: But the ladies and gentlemen who are watching would love
to—

EMILY: I said no. Read it yourself if it must be read.

DARWIN: Yes. By all means, do.

STEVE: Well, I feel *I* shouldn't be the one who . . . Oh, very well.
Wild Nights—Wild Nights!
Were I with thee
Wild nights should be
Our luxury!

Futile—the Winds—
To a Heart in port—
Done with the Compass—
Done with the Chart!

Rowing in Eden—
Ah, the Sea!
Might I but moor—Tonight—
In Thee!

DARWIN: Precisely. Now, surely the simple truth about the background of—

STEVE: Do you think men really want to hear the truth, Dr.
Darwin?

EMILY: We cannot take much of it at once, sir.
Tell all the Truth but tell it slant—
Success in Circuit lies
Too bright for our infirm Delight

The Truth's superb surprise.
As Lightning to the Children eased
With explanation kind
The Truth must dazzle gradually
Or every man be blind—

DARWIN: Quite so, my dear. To the extent that we are curious, it is only insofar as we might get a clearer insight into your remarkable verses.

STEVE: Did you travel much about New England?

EMILY: No. My home was my universe. After my father's death I never went outside the hedge that marked our property.

ATTILA: You didn't? Why not?

EMILY: I am not sure. Do we ever really understand why we do anything?

ATTILA: This is amazing. I roamed across the continent of Europe, and this woman chose to live in a world as small as one house.

EMILY: The last April my father lived . . . there were several snowstorms, and the birds were so frightened and cold they sat by the kitchen door.

Father went to the barn in slippers and came back with a breakfast of grain for each and hid himself when he scattered it, lest it embarrass them. Ignorant of the name or fate of their benefactor, their descendants are singing this afternoon.

But the sights and sounds and smells, the overwhelming importance of the personal relationships to which I was exposed in my home, were as much as I could bear.

I think perhaps I was born with too great a sensitivity. I responded to almost everything with some hidden lightning, and I think if I had gone again out into the world, with its thunder, its intrigues, its crimes, and clamors, I could not have defended myself against its onslaught.

So I remained within my own small universe. Now would you please ask me less personal questions!

STEVE: Very well. How do you feel about the women's liberation movement of today?

EMILY: Well, a child could see that certain of its particulars are long overdue. Obviously women deserve to be paid at the same rate as men if they do the same work. And no one, man or woman, should have less than equality before the law.

ATTILA: Maybe in this crazy country, but don't try to tell me that men and women are equal!

EMILY: The question was addressed to me, sir. But I must say that I do not understand what seems to have turned into a battle between the sexes in this country. I could visualize no higher calling than to be the joyous servant of an adored master, of a good, strong, and loving husband.

ATTILA: Well, that's more like it!

EMILY: *(She ignores the interruption, but is visibly annoyed.)* It would be utterly inconceivable to me to consider myself in all respects as equal. Ideally, it seems to me, a man and a woman should complement each other. They are not savage competitors for supremacy, but each provides a service the other desperately requires.

DARWIN: You do not mean only the physical?

EMILY: Not at all. I am talking about love. Until you have loved you have not met yourself. You have not known, really, who or what you are. For it is in the experience of love that we discover our virtues and our failings. If there is anything seriously wrong with us, it is in the attempt to relate to another that we will discover it. Love is the great revealer.

STEVE: Miss Dickinson, may we return to the subject of your poetry?

EMILY: *(Primly.)* Of my poetry, yes.

STEVE: I'll watch my step. Now you saw any one of your verses as a letter to the world, did you not?

EMILY: Yes. *(She lifts up a poem from the table.)*

> This is my letter to the World
> That never wrote to Me—
> The simple News that Nature told—
> With tender Majesty.
>
> Her Message is committed
> To Hands I cannot see;
> For love of Her—Sweet—countrymen—
> Judge tenderly—of Me

DARWIN: Would you advise all young poets to look for their inspiration in nature, in flowers, in trees, in clouds?

EMILY: *(She smiles.)* The true poets do not need to be advised. I issued this warning:

> Touch lightly Nature's sweet Guitar
> Unless thou knowest the Tune
> Or every Bird will point at thee
> Because a bard too soon—

ATTILA: Miss Dickinson, what is a poet?

EMILY: A trafficker with truth. Or, better yet, one in love with truth. He's quite as apt as any lover to be distorted in his view, but at least he respects his beloved.

DARWIN: Is there a connection, do you think, between poetry and madness?

EMILY: *(She gives him a strange look.)* Quite possibly, but remember:
Much Madness is divinest Sense—
To a discerning Eye—
Much Sense—the starkest Madness—
'Tis the Majority
In this, as All, prevail—
Assent—and you are sane—
Demur—you're straightway dangerous—
And handled with a Chain—

DARWIN: Why do you suppose it was, Miss Dickinson, that despite your present eminence as a poet, it took so long for American lovers of poetry to understand and appreciate you?

EMILY: I can only conjecture, Dr. Darwin. I would imagine my crime lay in being original.

DARWIN: Hear, hear.

EMILY: People really prefer not to be startled or informed or made to see things in new ways. What they really want, I fear, is the familiar. They bestow popularity, for the most part, as a reward for competent imitation, not originality.

DARWIN: Quite right. If you can manage to rephrase people's own prejudices in a comforting and familiar way, they may idolize you.

We see this even in the political arena. Many of the great statesmen and thinkers of history had to resist the most intense popular or institutional opposition. It is very dangerous to break through all the traditional boundaries.

STEVE: Yes, indeed.

We introduce again now the brilliant mathematician and physicist, who founded the science of dynamics in an age when previous scholars had studied matter in a static state.

He invented the thermometer, the telescope, and the hydro-static balance.

Ladies and gentlemen, Galileo Galilei. *(Galileo enters.)* *(Superimpose: Galileo Galilei, 1564–1642.)*

STEVE: Welcome back, sir.

GALILEO: Grazie, Signor.

STEVE: For the benefit of those who might have missed your last visit perhaps I should just mention here that you had told us of your difficulties with Church authorities who were alarmed by your discoveries.

GALILEO: Yes, this was because my studies showed that the earth was merely one small planet in boundless space. The churchmen considered that my crime was agreeing with Copernicus, who years earlier had pointed out that the sun, not the earth, was the center of our system.

EMILY: How in the world could it possibly have mattered if the earth was the center of the system, or was positioned somewhere else in space?

GALILEO: Well, today, Miss Dickinson, both scientists and philosophers, as well as theologians, realize that it doesn't matter at all. It never did, really. But the churchmen of my day thought it did.

DARWIN: And beliefs can be very powerful, Miss Dickinson, even when they are totally false.

STEVE: Well now, Signor Galileo, may I put a few questions to you about the education that prepared you for your remarkable scientific discoveries?

GALILEO: Good idea.

STEVE: Very well. Did you specialize in mathematics right from the start?

GALILEO: No. As a child I was lucky enough to be gifted in a number of areas so my family had some difficulty in making a choice. I wanted to become a mathematician.

STEVE: I imagine that made your father very happy.

GALILEO: Quite the contrary. He thought that mathematics was a waste of time.

STEVE: Waste of time!

DARWIN: Incredible!

GALILEO: Yes, he wanted me to become a physician.

STEVE: My son, the doctor, eh?

GALILEO: At seventeen I was entered in the University of Pisa. But I continued to study mathematics in secret, at least until my father found out what I was up to and became very angry.

STEVE: You know, it's most interesting.

You, sir, Miss Dickinson, and Dr. Darwin all had difficulty with domineering fathers.

ATTILA: My father, too, was no bargain.

STEVE: It's enough to make one suspect that the generation gap isn't a very recent discovery.

GALILEO: *(He laughs.)* Well, anyway, at the university I began to get myself into trouble by finding fault with the mathematics and physics of Aristotle. In fact, I argued with my teachers so frequently that they gave me the nickname of "the wrangler."

DARWIN: I think I should comment, Mr. Allen, on the astounding nature of what Signor Galileo did in attacking Aristotle.

There is in the modern world, for better or worse, no single philosopher or scientist who commands the incredible respect that Aristotle did in Europe, for many centuries.

Thomas Aquinas, the leading Catholic philosopher, himself considered Aristotle the philosopher par excellence. He was, in fact, an almost godlike figure to the scholars of Galileo's time.

STEVE: Oh, I see. In other words, to tangle with Aristotle was to put one's self in danger.

GALILEO: Well, in the long run it did add up to that, but not at first.

EMILY: When did you first begin to make your astounding scientific discoveries?

GALILEO: Well, Miss Dickinson, when I was nineteen years old I happened to notice one day, while in the Cathedral at Pisa, that there was a regularity, an order, to the arc of a hanging bronze lamp that someone had set swinging in the air.

STEVE: You mean the famous discovery you're telling us about was made when you were just a teen-ager?

GALILEO: Si, Signor. Well, I became tremendously excited when I noticed that although the arc of the swing was long at first, and then of course became shorter, nevertheless each swing of the lamp took exactly the same amount of time! *(He demonstrates with his hand.)*

DARWIN: This was really a scientific discovery of enormous importance!

GALILEO: Perhaps you're right, sir. But remember, I invented nothing here. I merely discovered one of Nature's magical laws, in action.

(He holds his pulse.) I used my pulse as a clock to measure the length of time of each swing, and at the same time it occurred to me that a device could be invented to measure the human pulse rate. I proceeded then to invent the pulselogia.

DARWIN: A really dazzling example of creative thinking! A man's mind grasping two separate parts of a situation and making two new discoveries at once.

GALILEO: Thank you, Dr. Darwin.

STEVE: You mentioned last week your disagreements with Aristotle. When was it that you finally disproved Aristotle's theory about falling bodies?

GALILEO: Well, after I left the university without receiving my doctor's degree—

STEVE: You did? Why was that?

GALILEO: Because I couldn't afford to pay for it. Anyway, like Dr. Darwin, I abandoned medicine and concentrated on geometry and mechanics. My work in these fields led me to receive a professorship at the university.

I then proceeded to demonstrate the error of Aristotle by the simple expedient of putting his theory to the test.

STEVE: You mean to say, Signor Galileo, that for thousands of years no one had ever thought to test Aristotle's theory?

GALILEO: Yes, sir, that's just what I mean. You see, for many centuries science was a branch of philosophy. Man's mind is indeed a powerful instrument and has worked many wonders, but it is also remarkably gifted at devising mountainous structures of error, fantasy, and all kinds of nonsense and falsehood.

But Aristotle had been right about so many things that even many scholars foolishly assumed he must be right about practically everything.

DARWIN: So it would have seemed rather an insult to his memory to have tested his scientific theories to see if they were correct.

GALILEO: Yes.

ATTILA: Then I see that it's possible to be both well educated and stupid at the same time.

GALILEO: I'm afraid so.

STEVE: Well, just how did you demonstrate that Aristotle was mistaken about falling bodies?

GALILEO: (He demonstrates with a large orange and a grape from a fruit bowl.) Well, to this day, I understand, most people think that if you drop, let's say, a cannonball and a lemon from a certain height that the cannonball, the heavier object, will hit the ground first.

ATTILA: It will.

GALILEO: No. You, and Aristotle, are mistaken. It seems reasonable, but it is not. The fact is, both objects will hit the ground at the same time, in ideal circumstances.

But the whole science of bodies falling through space, of matter in motion, is incredibly fascinating. Let me give you another illustration.

Suppose we shoot a bullet at a very small target, oh, let's say, two hundred feet away. We aim the bullet in a perfectly straight line, horizontally. Now, when will the bullet hit the target if it is traveling, let us assume, at two hundred feet per second?

STEVE: Well, I suppose it would reach the target in one second.

GALILEO: No. The bullet will *never* reach the target.

STEVE: Never? Why not?

GALILEO: Because of gravity, which will pull it down to pass below the target.

This applies, needless to say, regardless of the speed of the bullet and the distance of the target if we consider the question in ideal terms.

Let me give you another illustration. Let's say we have two cannonballs, all right? Now one of them we shoot from a cannon horizontally at a very high rate of speed. It falls to the ground, let us say, half a mile away. The second cannonball we simply drop straight down, from the same height.

Now, which one will hit the ground first?

STEVE: Well, I would think the one that is dropped would reach the ground first. It travels such a short distance.

ATTILA: No. Because the one fired from the cannon would be going so fast, I say it would reach the ground first.

GALILEO: You have forgotten our first illustration, gentlemen. The fact is the two objects would hit the ground at the same time.

In other words, the horizontal velocity is independent of the vertical velocity. Both cannonballs are pulled down by gravity at the same rate, by the same force. I proved this by dropping objects of different weights from the top of the Leaning Tower of Pisa.

ATTILA: Did your pointing out the errors of Aristotle make you a great hero, Galileo?

GALILEO: (*He laughs.*) I'm afraid not. Other scholars were furious. The feeling against me became so intense that I was actually forced to resign from the university. So I moved on to another post, at the University of Padua.

DARWIN: It was at Padua that you began to seriously study the heavens, wasn't it?

GALILEO: Yes. The planets, the stars, fascinated me! I gave thought to the view of Copernicus, who had said that the sun, not the earth, was the center of the universe.

We now know that there is no true *center* of the universe, since we do not even know the dimensions of the universe.

But Copernicus was right in that the sun is the center of our planetary system. The earth is only a tiny ball revolving around the sun. But the sun itself also moves through an enormous orbit in space.

My lectures on astronomy were so popular at Padua that many hundreds of people would crowd in to hear them.

By the use of the telescope—I was one of several people who invented the telescope, by the way—I saw that the surface of the moon had mountains and craters and that there were not just a few thousand but many millions and millions of stars.

DARWIN: And all these discoveries alarmed the Church greatly?

GALILEO: Yes. The Pope himself called me to Rome for questioning, and four times I was called before the Holy Inquisition, as I explained last week.

EMILY: How infuriating!

GALILEO: You see, the Church felt that everything in the heavens had to revolve around the earth simply because it was the planet on which Christ had been born.

ATTILA: I have nothing against Christ, but that's the stupidest reasoning I ever heard of!

GALILEO: *(He laughs heartily.)* Well, at last, under fearful pressure from the Inquisition, I agreed to stop teaching that the earth moved through space.

EMILY: Dreadful.

STEVE: Signor Galileo, there's a famous story that at this particular moment you muttered to yourself, *"E pur si muove."* And still it moves.

Some historians accept the story and others say it is not factual. Could you enlighten us on that?

GALILEO: To tell you the truth, I honestly don't remember whether I said that. There's no doubt that I *thought* it because I was perfectly aware that the earth moves; but what I might have muttered under my breath at that moment, if indeed I muttered anything *(he shrugs)*, after so long a time, who can say? Does anyone present recall with certainty everything he muttered even one week ago?

EMILY: Well, anyway, you were right to oppose the Church in this matter.

GALILEO: Thank you, Miss Dickinson. But may I point out that I always remained loyal to the Church. I never left it.

But enough of me. I'd like to hear more about Darwin's ideas.

STEVE: Dr. Darwin, last week you gave us the general idea of your theory of evolution.

DARWIN: Yes, I think we had got to about 1842 in my story.

Well, 1842 was rather a happy year for me. After publishing a report of my five-year voyage on the *Beagle*, I married my dear cousin, Emma Wedgwood.

As I've mentioned she was of the prominent pottery family, which produced Wedgwood china.

EMILY: Oh, yes.

DARWIN: Perhaps the later criticisms my work received did not wound me as much as might otherwise have been the case because I was able to work in the peace, comfort, and security of a very happy home.

My wife Emma bore me ten children, and although we suffered the tragedy of seeing three die in childhood, the rest were loving and affectionate.

I don't really know that I could have worked as successfully as I did without the security that my home gave me.

EMILY: How lovely.

DARWIN: Yes. Well, this is important because my married life, I think, gave me back a security that had been undermined by my father. He had said to me, "Charles, you'll never amount to anything. All you care about is animals."

And, you know, that sort of blow cuts very deeply. I adored my mother, a marvelous woman—a Unitarian, incidentally—but she died when I was only six.

STEVE: So you told us last week that your round-the-world voyage taught you a great deal about the realities of the animal world.

DARWIN: Precisely. Then later when I read the works of Malthus, I realized that Malthus had discovered a great, though disturbing, truth.

STEVE: Which was?

DARWIN: That *man* can take certain measures to increase his food supply. Or he can diminish his numbers, by restraint from marriage, or by other means. But the animal and vegetable kingdoms are unable to take such measures. Therefore they reproduce to the limit, but are always faced with a strictly limited means of subsistence. Consequently vast numbers of them fall in death and starvation by the wayside, and in this fierce struggle victory goes to the organism best adapted to its surroundings.

STEVE: So at certain times there is not enough food to go around.

DARWIN: Yes, and it is the struggle for this food—the struggle for existence—that means that favorable variations, however seemingly insignificant, will tend to help an individual of the species to survive; and therefore these variations will be preserved in future generations, while unfavorable variations will gradually disappear.

ATTILA: Can you give us an example?

DARWIN: Certainly. Suppose a certain kind of bear inhabits a forest range. Then suppose an ice age begins to develop. Now a few bears are going to be born with, let us say, relatively thinner coats of fur, and others may be born with thicker coats of fur, or perhaps thicker layers of fat.

It is obvious that if the average temperatures drop to a certain point, then the bears with the thicker protective coats are more likely to survive. And since they do survive, and reproduce their kind, then this will gradually lead to more and more bears with thicker coats being born.

GALILEO: So eventually *all* the bears of this particular hypothetical species may have thick coats.

DARWIN: Yes. That, in simplified form anyway, is the idea of "natural selection" and "the survival of the fittest."

ATTILA: Well, now, even in my day, Darwin, we could see that if two overweight people married they would tend to have overweight children.

And we also knew that a strong muscular man would be likely to have strong muscular children.

DARWIN: You're not quite right, my friend, on that last point. It *is* true that the physical characteristics of parents will appear in their children, at least if they have enough children; but we now know that acquired characteristics are not transmitted genetically.

ATTILA: What the hell does that mean?

DARWIN: Well, for many thousands of years people supposed that if a man exercised and developed enormously powerful muscles, this *acquired* characteristic, well-developed musculature, could be transmitted to his children.

I suppose the reason this mistake was made was that it often happens that children will *imitate* the ways of their parents.

Therefore, if a man were particularly athletic, it might well be that purely by *social imitation* his sons and daughters, too, would do what was necessary to develop their bodies. But physical inheritance has nothing whatever to do with the matter.

But you should not feel the least bit uncomfortable, Attila, in holding such a view because even in the present day, I understand, there are those who think it reasonable. As a matter of fact I am told that even in the modern Soviet Union a scientist named Lysenko developed a theory of genetics and evolution which was officially approved by the government, based on precisely the error that I've just pointed out to you.

One of the reasons it has been so difficult for even specialists to perceive the workings of evolution, is that most of the physical changes that have taken place in species have taken hundreds of thousands or millions of years to develop.

STEVE: But aren't there some instances, in the case of simpler life-forms, where reproduction takes place so often that we can actually *see* the evolutionary process take place, in a very short time-span?

DARWIN: Thank goodness, yes. Here in the United States in recent years, I am told, a biologist named Demerec grew a certain bacteria in cultures that contained the drug streptomycin. Now streptomycin is fatal to this particular bacteria. It is a poison to them. Nevertheless Demerec made the astounding discovery that after the passage of some time, the strain of bacteria became totally resistant to streptomycin and was no longer poisoned or harmed by it!

He discovered that this remarkable effect was not due to the bacteria individually becoming more resistant but simply to the presence of a few individual freaks or mutants which, purely by accident, happened to be resistant to the streptomycin which poisoned the other bacteria.

GALILEO: So then the resistant mutants were the only ones that could survive and multiply?

DARWIN: Exactly! All the normal bacteria were killed off, and so in a very short time only the mutants were left! We can see all this because bacteria multiply so fast.

STEVE: Yes. Well, I suppose that's about all they've got to do.

ATTILA: Well, now that you explain your theories I admit that there does seem to be something to them. I can see, after all, how due to certain circumstances of climate, or whatever, a kind of fish might develop a more powerful tail, or a breed of turtle might develop a harder shell; but I'll be damned if I can see how really big changes can take place!

Are you trying to tell me that this thing you call evolution can change a frog's leg into the wing of a bird?

DARWIN: Well, what I meant was that—

ATTILA: Do you tell me it can gradually change some kind of a fish into something like a rabbit or a horse? No, Darwin, I have the feeling that you're asking us to believe far too much.

DARWIN: Your question is quite a respectable one, my friend. What you are talking about here refers to degrees of probability. And you are absolutely right. Mathematically speaking it is highly improbable that such things have taken place. And yet, I assure you, they have.

GALILEO: I would think that the explanation of the mystery lies in the factor of time.

DARWIN: Precisely! Each individual change may be very slight indeed, although some changes are rather dramatic. These mutations, as they are called, represent the big steps in the evolutionary process. But time, as I say, is all important.

You see, there is a sense in which *all* living things are of equal age. They can all trace their original simple ancestry back perhaps five hundred million years along the stream of time.

So it is *that* comparatively long period that has made all the millions of small genetic changes add up to the variety of species we see about us.

EMILY: But how can you be so certain, Dr. Darwin, that our ancestors are so old?

DARWIN: Well, Miss Dickinson, that was just the question that was so troubling to people who believed that God had made the world in six 24-hour periods, only about five thousand years ago.

But you see, we have found fossil remains of primitive *men* that go back to a time about two million years ago!

ATTILA: Two million?

DARWIN: Yes! Certain animals that look rather like our modern crabs have been located in the fossil stage in rocks that man now knows are almost five hundred million years old.

One very important thing we learn from these fossils is that fish emerged on this planet in the water before amphibians, that amphibians were on the earth before reptiles, that reptiles lived before birds, etc. Scientists now believe that all this evidence shows that biological life has developed from one simple form, through a series of ever more complex forms.

ATTILA: But wait a minute, Darwin. How do things that live under the water—fishes and things like that—how do they breathe?

DARWIN: By means of organs called gills. They are the equivalent of the lungs with which the dry-land animals breathe.

ATTILA: All right. Now if you're trying to tell me that over some long period of time some animals that lived in the water finally developed into land animals, then you tell me this. When those gills of the fishes were changing into the lungs of seals, or any other land animals, was there some period of time when these creatures had a combination of one gill and one lung, or two organs that were half gills and half lungs?

DARWIN: My friend, you raise a perfectly fair question, and it's a question that has concerned scientists for a good many years. First of all I must explain that in outlining a theory it is not necessary that one know everything that could possibly be known about the particular field of science involved. No one man in his lifetime could possibly acquire such a great body of knowledge anyway. So the simple fact that we evolutionists have not answered every conceivable question about evolution does not mean we should abandon all the important discoveries we *have* made, and all the important facts we have clearly established.

Now, as regards the specific question you raise, perhaps the answer is contained in the life processes of that common creature of quite a different kind, which, in the English language anyway, we call a tadpole. Now the tadpole is spawned like a fish. He is hatched and lives in water like a fish. He has gills like a fish. And this certainly seems to establish the fact of his fishlike ancestry.

But as he grows a remarkable thing happens! He gradually absorbs his tail. He starts to put forth little legs. He gradually loses his gills, which is to say, nature performs in him exactly the sort of miracle that you have suggested could not possibly happen. He develops lungs, he hops out onto land and from that moment is just as much an air breather as a horse, a dog, or a man. So here, you see, in the life of this amphibian creature, may be recapitulated the mysterious change of early water species into what have become the land dwellers of today.

I believe it will be also relevant to draw your attention to the fact that man himself, during the first nine months of his existence, is, in a certain sense, not a dry-land creature but lives in a watery environment. There is no air in the womb, you know.

Another support for my theory came after my time when it occurred to biologists studying embryology.

STEVE: Embryology?

DARWIN: Yes, the growth of new living organisms from *eggs*. It was learned that in the development of many living creatures there is a stage when the *embryo* is very much like a fish. Then later there is a stage when it strikingly resembles an amphibian, after which it passes through a reptile stage, before reaching its final form, as, say, a cow or a man.

A third indication that my theories were reliable is in the remarkable similarity of the skeletal structures of living animals. For example, if we compare the bone structure in the paddles of a turtle, the flippers of a whale or seal, the wings of a bird, the front legs of a four-legged animal, the arms of a man, the surprising thing we discover is that all these bone structures are very much alike.

ATTILA: *(He looks at his arm and hand.)* My arm is like that of an animal?

EMILY: I would say so.

DARWIN: A fourth strong support for my theories is that you and I have organs in our bodies today which are of no apparent use whatever.

STEVE: Such as?

DARWIN: Well, the appendix, for one.

Since nature does seem to have a reasonable impulse to it, it is unlikely that man was created with these useless organs.

What seems much more likely is that these organs are vestigial relics handed down from our earlier ancestors. They originally had a use but are no longer necessary to our health or survival.

STEVE: Well, that's fascinating.

EMILY: It certainly is. Er . . . Dr. Darwin, I was wondering just when your troubles with the churches started.

DARWIN: Well, when the Association for the Advancement of Science met in Oxford, that was in 1860, I believe, Bishop Wilberforce, who because he was also a mathematician imagined

himself a man of science, publicly announced that he was going
to "smash Darwin."

EMILY: Oh, my goodness.

DARWIN: Unfortunately I was not present to witness the destruction, but reports have since circulated concerning the Bishop's
confrontation with the eminent scientist Thomas Huxley.

Bishop Wilberforce begged to know was it through his *grandfather* or his *grandmother* that Huxley claimed his descent from a
monkey?

A written transcript of Huxley's reply was not made at the
time, but because his words were so dramatic they have been
reconstituted by one who was present.

EMILY: Do tell us what he said!

DARWIN: Since I've always relished his response I have a copy of it
here with me. (*He opens a folded paper.*)

In reply to the Bishop's insulting question, Mr. Huxley said,
quote:

> A man has no reason to be ashamed of having had an *ape* for his
> grandfather. If there were an ancestor whom I should feel shame
> in recalling, it would be rather a *man*, a man of restless and
> versatile *intellect*, who not content with success in his own
> sphere of activity, plunges into scientific questions with which
> he has *no* real acquaintance, only to obscure them by an endless
> rhetoric, and distract the attention of his hearers from the real
> point at issue, by eloquent digression and skilled appeals to
> religious prejudice.

STEVE: Remarkable.

DARWIN: Oh, one last thought about evolution. Sometimes even
people to whom it seems a reasonable theory imagine that it
involves things that happened millions of years ago. That is
quite true, but it misses the central point by a rather wide
margin. Evolution *started* at the moment of *creation*, has never
stopped, and will never stop so long as there is life on this
planet!

STEVE: Dr. Darwin, you were kind enough to read to us the
famous reply of Dr. Huxley. I wonder if you would also be good
enough to read the justifiably famous passage from the last paragraph of your book *The Origin of Species*.

DARWIN: Certainly, Mr. Allen. I will be glad to oblige.

STEVE: (*He speaks while Darwin is turning the pages of his book.*) You might be particularly interested in this passage, Miss Dickinson, in that it seems to have a poetic tone to it.

EMILY: Is that right? *(She listens attentively.)*

DARWIN: *(Reading.)*

> It is interesting to contemplate a tangled bank, clothed with many plants of many kinds—with birds singing on the bushes, with various insects flitting about, and with worms crawling through the damp earth—and to reflect that these elaborately constructed forms, so different from each other in so complex a number, have all been produced by laws acting around us.
>
> These laws, taken in the largest sense *(he counts them off with his five fingers)*, being: *growth with reproduction; inheritance*, which is almost implied by reproduction; *variability*, from the indirect and direct action of the conditions of life, and from use and disuse; a *ratio of increase* so high as to lead to a struggle for life and, as a consequence, to *natural selection*, entailing the *extinction of less-improved forms*.
>
> Thus, from the *war of nature*, from *famine* and *death*, the most exalted object which we are capable of conceiving, namely, the production of the higher animals, directly follows.
>
> There is grandeur in this view of life . . . that whilst this planet has gone cycling on according to the fixed law of gravity, from so simple a beginning, endless forms most beautiful and most wonderful, are being yet evolved.

GALILEO: The poetry in that passage, Dr. Darwin, shows us that your reverence for Nature was in some ways similar to Miss Dickinson's.

EMILY: Yes, Dr. Darwin. Your words remind me that . . .

> To make a prairie it takes a clover and one bee,
> One clover, and a bee,
> And revery.
> The revery alone will do,
> If bees are few.

STEVE: Miss Dickinson, do you think it possible that your dependence on Nature was partly a way of comforting yourself after the blows that life dealt to you?

EMILY: No, I always loved Nature, even as a child. But at the end of my life even natural beauty was too painful. Even the trees, the grass, the woodland creatures that I loved, because of their beauty, held terror for me. *(She searches among her papers, finds, and reads:)*

I dreaded that first Robin, so,
But He is mastered, now,
I've some accustomed to Him grown,
He hurts a little, though—

I thought if I could only live
Till that first Shout got by—
Not all Pianos in the Woods
Had power to mangle me—

I dared not meet the Daffodils—
For fear their Yellow Gown
Would pierce me with a fashion
So foreign to my own—

I wished the Grass would hurry—
So—when 'twas time to see—
He'd be too tall, the tallest one
Could stretch—to look at me—

I could not bear the Bees should come,
I wished they'd stay away
In those dim countries where they go,
What word had they, for me?

They're here, though; not a creature failed—
No Blossom stayed away
In gentle deference to me—
The Queen of Calvary—

Each one salutes me, as he goes,
And I, my childish Plumes,
Lift, in bereaved acknowledgment
Of their unthinking Drums—

ATTILA: I've heard just about enough of this nonsense about nature! You said in one of your poems that it's wrong to kill a bird?
Then you must think it's wrong to kill any animal.

EMILY: Yes, I—

ATTILA: *(He looks under the table.)* You're wearing shoes, aren't you,
lady? I see they're made of leather. How do you think the
shoemakers got that leather? By asking a steer if they could

borrow it? No, they *slaughtered* that animal and they *robbed* him of his leather. And you're all damned lucky they did or you might be walking around in bare feet, which can be pretty inconvenient in the cold of winter.

What about your eating habits? Don't you ever eat eggs? Do you drink milk? Do you eat beef?

GALILEO: Well, some people are vegetarians and I don't believe the—

ATTILA: Sure, they are. But I doubt if one man in a thousand lives only by eating plants and seeds. But the vegetarians at least are consistent. The rest of you are a bunch of hypocrites, enjoying your tearful poems about birds and beautiful animals on the one hand and then participating in the slaughter of these same creatures on the other.

And I think the pretty lady here is confusing us with her overly sentimental attitudes about death.

Death is inevitable, isn't it? It's part of the natural order. If the kind of God you three believe in still has anything to do with running the universe, then He must have established death as something just as natural as birth, as life itself.

It seems to me you've all become soft and spineless. In my time death was something we saw almost every day. We had no medicine worth talking about. We had no way to kill pain. We had no way to mend broken bones. We were attacked by floods, famine, diseases, lightning, wild animals, our neighbors, the armies of our enemies. We lived daily in the presence of death.

So you either adjusted yourself to the situation and became one of the victors—

EMILY: One of the killers, you mean.

ATTILA: That's right. It was either kill or be killed, as it is in the world of Nature that Darwin has described to us.

I can't help being infuriated when I hear all this weak-kneed talk about love, nature, death, and all the rest of it. For God's sake, Darwin, were you so busy counting and weighing your specimens that you didn't look at the true nature of their existence?

DARWIN: Oh, no sir. I remind you that I always insisted on the struggle for survival. Nature is incredibly wasteful. A thousand living creatures will die that one may live. Living organisms survive largely by destroying the life of others.

ATTILA: You're damned right! Under every wave, behind every

bush, under every inch of soil, in every forest and jungle and meadow in the world, down through all time and at this very moment the whole *planet* is drenched with blood!

Creatures in the wild don't die peacefully in their beds, my friend. They usually die in agony, eaten alive by some other, larger creature. The very animals and bees and birds that you write your sappy poems about, lady, themselves live by stealing the food they need from creatures beneath themselves.

You write a poem, Miss Dickinson, about a bird hopping down a garden path, and you get all dewy-eyed about the beauty of the bird. But what about the angleworm that he swallowed alive?

This whole stinking world, I repeat, is drenched in blood at this very moment, as it has always been, and as it will always be.

DARWIN: You are quite right, Attila. But the animals can do nothing to improve the dangerous conditions of their lives. Man is different. Man *can*, by giving thoughtful attention to the problem, improve the conditions of his existence.

EMILY: Yes.

ATTILA: Sure, but for the most part all he does is try to make himself more comfortable.

He invents ways to keep himself warm. He makes soft pillows and beds to lie in, he builds houses to keep the rain off his head. But as I look around the world today I don't see nearly as much evidence that man has become, in any important respect, more civilized.

The only difference *I* note is he's become more cowardly, even in the way he kills. He now does it long distance, not hand to hand.

GALILEO: But my good sir, with the advent of Christianity, there were certain important changes that—

ATTILA: Christianity? Don't make me laugh! I'm no strange visitor from another planet, Galileo! I lived in the fifth century when Christianity was dominant and powerful throughout Europe. I never saw any wild tribes that were more adept than the good Christians at massacring each other. There were a few saintly Christians in my day, I grant you. But damned few!

And look at the situation today. The Christians of Ireland have been slaughtering each other for centuries, and recently they've got on to it again. And the good Christians of America dropped what you call your atomic bombs on two cities in Japan in which, I understand, a great many Christians happened to live.

I don't attack Christ Himself. Human life would be far better if it were conducted according to His principles. It would certainly put a stop to the bloodshed. Though, come to think of it, I'm told He *did* say that He came not to bring peace but a sword.

GALILEO: Yes. I've never understood that.

ATTILA: But show me the tribe, show me the city, show me the nation that has ever actually conducted its affairs on peaceful Christian principles!

You people preach "Blessed are the peacemakers." But let a man dedicate his life to the cause of peace, when you would rather continue with the business of slaughtering your enemy, and see what happens to that peacemaker. Do you *bless* him? Don't make me laugh. You usually call him a traitor and throw him in jail, if not a lot worse.

But (*he laughs suddenly*) perhaps I shouldn't be so hard on the Christians. After all, they made it easier for me to conquer the Roman Empire since they had thrown it into such weakness and confusion.

STEVE: I think St. Augustine, Bishop of Hippo, would differ with you on that point, Attila. Perhaps he'll join us on one of our future discussions.

Now perhaps we'd better change the subject. I'm sorry, Miss Dickinson.

EMILY: That's quite all right.

DARWIN: You never married, did you, Miss Dickinson?

EMILY: I am Miss Dickinson, Dr. Darwin.

DARWIN: Oh, quite.

GALILEO: But you wrote many love poems.

EMILY: I did. And to satisfy your idle curiosity at last, gentlemen, they were based on that out of which every true poet constructs his verses, the pain of lived experience. Fortunately . . .

We outgrow love, like other things,
And put it in the Drawer—
Till it in emptied fashion shows,
Like costumes grandsires wore.

STEVE: But, before love dies it lives! If I may say so, Miss Dickinson, two of your love poems are among my personal favorites.

Would you read for us, please, "If You Were Coming in the Fall"?

EMILY: Very well.

> If you were coming in the Fall,
> I'd brush the Summer by
> With half a smile, and half a spurn,
> As Housewives do, a Fly.
>
> If I could see you in a year,
> I'd wind the months in balls—
> And put them each in separate Drawers,
> Until their time befalls.
>
> If only Centuries, delayed,
> I'd count them on my Hand,
> Subtracting, till my fingers dropped
> Into Van Diemen's Land.
>
> If certain, when this life was out—
> That yours and mine should be
> I'd toss it yonder, like a Rind,
> And take Eternity—
>
> But, now, all ignorant of the length,
> of time's uncertain wing,
> It goads me, like the Goblin Bee—
> That will not state—its sting.

STEVE: Miss Dickinson, forgive me, but of your millions of admirers, a few now believe that the man to whom you wrote those beautiful words . . . was the Reverend Charles Wadsworth of Philadelphia.

EMILY: Oh, why must you—(She weeps.)

DARWIN: (He hurries to console her.) But, don't you see, dear lady, out of your suffering and pain . . . out of your loss . . . has come the most incredible *beauty* . . . for all the world.

From the tragic fact that the Reverend Wadsworth was a married man . . . and that each of you denied yourself the pleasure of the other. From all that . . . came such beauty as you poured into this poem.

We will understand it now . . . at last . . . if you read it to us. (He hands her another poem.)

EMILY: Must I?

GALILEO: Please.

EMILY: I cannot live with You—
It would be Life—
And Life is over there—
Behind the shelf

The Sexton keeps the Key to—
Putting up
Our Life—His porcelain—
Like a cup—

Discarded of the Housewife—
Quaint—or Broken—
A newer Sèvres pleases—
Old Ones crack—

I could not die—with You—
For One must wait
To shut the Other's Gaze down—
You—could not—

And I—Could stand by
And see You—freeze—
Without my Right of Frost—
Death's privilege?

Nor could I rise—with You—
Because Your Face
Would put out Jesus'—
That New Grace

Glow plain—and foreign
On my homesick Eye—
Except that You than He
Shone closer by—

They'd judge Us—How—
For You—served Heaven—You know,
Or sought to—
I could not—

Because you saturated sight—
And I had no more Eyes
For sordid excellence
As Paradise

And were You lost, I would be—
Though My Name
Rang loudest
On the Heavenly fame—

And were You—saved—
And I—condemned to be
Where You were not—
That self—were Hell to Me—

So We must keep apart—
You there—I here—
With just the Door ajar
That oceans are—and Prayer—
And that Pale Sustenance, Despair.

DARWIN: Now, you see, we understand the reason for your withdrawal from the world. The reason for your seclusion. The reason for your fascination with death.

EMILY: Thank you, sir. And yet . . . my withdrawal was in the direction of creativity and faith. *(She reads.)*

If I shouldn't be alive
When the Robins come,
Give the one in Red Cravat,
A Memorial crumb.

If I couldn't thank you,
Being just asleep,
You will know I'm trying
With my Granite lip!

GALILEO: You mentioned faith.

EMILY: Yes.

I never saw a Moor,
I never saw the Sea—
Yet know I how the Heather looks
And what a wave must be.

I never spoke with God
Nor visited in Heaven—
Yet certain am I of the spot
As if the chart were given—

Going to Heaven!
I don't know when—
Pray do not ask me how!
Indeed I'm too astonished
To think of answering you!
Going to Heaven!
How dim it sounds!
And yet it will be done
As sure as flocks go home at night
Unto the Shepherd's arm!

Perhaps you're going too!
Who knows?
If you should get there first,
Save just a little place for me
Close to the two I lost—
The smallest "Robe" will fit me
And just a bit of "Crown"—
For you know we do not mind our dress
When we are going home—

STEVE: Thank you, Miss Dickinson, gentlemen. Unfortunately we've run out of time. Thank you all so much for visiting with us.